*Patricia Phillips dedicates this to her husband, John,
and children, Toni, Lisa, Paul, Samantha, and John.*

*George Mair dedicates this to his late wife,
Carolinda Haverlin Mair.*

CONTENTS

ABOUT THE AUTHORS

Patricia Phillips is a lawyer specializing in the area of Family Law and Mediation. Ms. Phillips is a Fellow of the American Academy of Matrimonial Lawyers and is a Family Law Specialist certified by the State Bar of California. She is a member of the Family Law Sections of the Los Angeles County Bar Association, the State Bar of California, and the American Bar Association, and has written and lectured extensively in the area of Family Law and Mediation.

In addition to her activities in the Family Law Bar, Ms. Phillips was the first woman president of the Los Angeles County Bar Association and is a former member of the Board of Governors of the State Bar of California. Currently, Ms. Phillips serves as the chair of the State Bar Commission on the Future of the Legal Profession and the State Bar, which is charged with anticipating the future legal needs of the public and the ability of the legal profession to meet those needs.

Ms. Phillips is married to John T. Phillips, M.D., and they are the parents of five adult children.

George Mair was an editorial director with CBS and a *Los Angeles Times* nationally syndicated columnist for fifteen years before becoming press secretary to the Speaker of the House of Representatives and a radio talk-show host in Washington, D.C.

He has sixteen books to his credit. His latest book is a hardcover biography, *Oprah: The Real Story*. Mair is a widower who spends his time at the beach in Malibu when not writing.

THANK YOU DOESN'T
SEEM LIKE ENOUGH . . .

. . . for those people who have helped us in creating this book, which we hope will provide happiness and financial security for many women everywhere.

Meanwhile, our thanks go out to . . .

Bert Holtje, an extraordinary literary agent whose patience, good nature, and insight were essential in creating this book.

Barbara Gilson at Macmillan, who conceived the idea for this book to help women faced with divorce and then had the faith to put it in our hands for implementation.

CHAPTER ONE

Bad Divorces Happen to Nice Women

Being rich and famous can protect you from many things, but not from a bad divorce. Too often women with power, money, and stature still are mauled in a bad divorce. We start with a look at some of these women who have endured a bad divorce, even though they began the process much better off than most women. No matter how rich and powerful they were, they didn't prepare themselves for divorce and they came out relatively poorly. If women with such ample resources can be victimized by a divorce, imagine what can happen to you. That is why this book is important to all women, regardless of wealth or position.

Some wealthy women have done well financially. Soraya Khashoggi received $800 million in her divorce from international arms dealers Adnan Khashoggi; Anne Bass was awarded $200 million in her divorce from Sid. Frances Lear concluded life with Norman with $112 million, which she used to start *Lear's* magazine. And the $100 million Amy Irving took from her divorce from Steven Spielberg was not peanuts.

However, don't let a few million dollars blind you to what happened in some of these cases. These settlements have to be placed in context of the collective wealth of the families. For example, take the divorce in 1991 between Patricia and John Kluge in Virginia. Kluge is one of the richest men in the world. The publicized story was that Pat Kluge got a settlement of a fine Virginia estate, Albemarle House, and $8 million. That is not much from a man worth over a billion dollars, but it is even less when you examine it closely. She did not get $8 million—only the annual interest on $8 million, with the principal reverting to Kluge upon the occurrence of certain conditions. She also did not receive Albemarle House, but only the *use* of it for some years. Both Albemarle House and the $8 million remain John's, and Pat has only the temporary use of them. Thus, for her lifetime, in a sense, she remains under the control of the man she has divorced.

How was this result possible? Apparently John Kluge is a decisive man who moved quickly to protect himself and his assets when his marriage was disintegrating. While the Kluge divorce was front-page material, both the press and most other observers missed the key to the lopsided settlement: The minute John and Patricia separated, John jetted to Mexico and obtained a divorce, and the Virginia divorce, months later, was their *second* divorce. What is the point of that move by Kluge? While there is some question as to the legality of the Mexican divorce, it created an issue that would delay the inevitable. To settle the issue created by the potentially invalid Mexican divorce would have required court hearings and, after appeals, more court hearings to the point that the final divorce might be delayed several years. Long, drawn-out court battles are something wealthy spouses *and* their wives, in some instances, generally want to avoid because the wealthy spouse can afford it and the other spouse cannot, because the stakes are too high, or perhaps because the alternative offer is good enough to make the battle less appealing. In giving advice to husbands involved in divorce, the September 1991 issue of *M, Inc.* magazine noted, "While the wife may stand to get a sizable alimony and a healthy property settlement after the case is settled, for the time being she could very well be broke. A hardball approach to her desperate straits would be to threaten to hold out through a long divorce proceeding, even through appeals, without settling. Since the husband knows that he is unlikely to lose more than half of his holdings no matter how long the divorce takes and he will have use of his cash in the meantime, it is definitely to his advantage to hold out."

There are a number of ways that the husband, particularly if he is the major income earner, can play hardball during a divorce. Most attorneys will advise husbands who believe their marriage is destined for divorce court to file for the divorce as early as possible, because each passing year may raise their earning potential and increase the value of the settlement they will have to pay. Generally, the key to a successful financial settlement is preparation by hiring an accountant, who may use a variety of innovative accounting devices to depress the value of the estate to be divided, create a new set of books, undervalue the property, and segregate the property to enable the husband to claim that it was his before marriage. The wife can counter that tactic with experts of her own. But expert testimony is expensive, adds to the cost of the divorce for both spouses, and could price it out of the wife's ability to pay. In that case, she may have to settle for much less because she cannot afford to mount an adequate counterattack. In most jurisdictions, however, the wealthy spouse will be ordered to advance funds to enable the wife to hire competent counsel and experts. Still, the spouse in control of the money can spend what he thinks is necessary. You will have to justify your need for funds to the court.

Levering a woman's emotions against her can also work to the husband's advantage. For example, threatening a knockdown, drag-out battle over custody of the children is draining emotionally and financially and is a ploy that many husbands—even those who have no intention of taking the children—often use as a lever. Believe it or not, some husbands have introduced a younger girlfriend into the situation even when she is a ringer. (You can be sure it will not take much to change that charade into the real thing.) Most wives regard this behavior with rage and act irrationally, which makes them appear foolish to the court and, sometimes, to their own attorney. Such behavior is not helpful to their cases, in any event.

Divorces often take longer than you anticipate. Sustaining yourself during the divorce proceedings may be difficult. However, take heart that your divorce will not take as long as that of C. B. and Marcella Schetter of Broward County, Florida, which was originally filed when Lyndon Johnson was president in December 1966 and was finally settled May 19, 1993—over twenty-six years later. The case lasted through two judges, several attorneys, and C. B. Schetter himself. He died in 1986.

As women begin to earn better salaries, the tables may be turned. TV's Joan Lunden of *Good Morning, America* certainly was not happy about being liberated when she was ordered to pay her estranged house husband, Michael Krauss, $18,000 a month in temporary alimony.

The objective of this book is to level the playing field. Our goal is to prepare you to win in the divorce contest and to avoid the costly and painful pitfalls common in contemporary divorce.

Older women who have invested much of their lives, energies, and souls in a long marriage too frequently are taken advantage of and destroyed emotionally and financially by a divorce.

This devastation may be due to the enormous resistance of some women to approaching their life situation realistically. Some are insecure and lack the determination and know-how to obtain a fair shake in the divorce. Another of our goals is to help you learn to approach your situation with your eyes open.

For example, even *before marriage* divorce is a dirty word; women need to embrace more than their husband-to-be. They need to embrace an age-old English and Latin tradition of the marriage contract, which we will discuss later.

We do not advocate divorce. Neither do we advocate major surgery or rape. To the contrary, we hope you are never faced with any of these incidents. However, we do know that one way of avoiding devastating divorce, major surgery, or rape is to prepare yourself. Be alert for the danger signs so you can avoid these assaults. At least you can minimize the detrimental effect divorce will inevitably have on your life.

When it becomes clear that divorce is unavoidable, you should know how to play one of the most vicious, unfair, hardball games in our American culture. Your success is critical not only for yourself but for your children, and will dictate the way the rest of your life will be lived.

To understand the problem of women who enter divorce unprepared and unprotected, you need only contemplate what has happened to women married to powerful and wealthy men who are not prepared to face and meet the realities of the dissolution of their marriage.

Johnny Carson, one of the richest men in Hollywood, has had several wives. The last one he divorced received a generous settlement that will provide her with a lifetime of comfortable living, while Johnny's first wife, according to press reports, today lives in poverty.

Jack Kent Cooke divorced his first wife and gave her what was then the largest settlement in history (it was even listed in the *Guinness Book of Records*). The last woman Cooke divorced, Marlene Cooke, bore him a daughter but received virtually nothing in the divorce and had to sue Cooke to obtain support for their child. Why would one of the richest men in the world be unwilling to support his own child? Anybody who knows Jack Kent Cooke will tell you the issue is not money. The issue with him, as it is with many men, is control. Many a man continues to control his former wife's destiny long after the divorce by control of her purse strings and by limiting her right to relocate when their children are in her custody.

Your best protection is to anticipate the issues and prepare for them. That's what this book helps you do. It will help you emerge from the divorce process a winner and assure you a decent future.

CHAPTER TWO

Think About Divorce Before You Get Married

While this title may sound somewhat cynical, we advise that you prepare yourself for whatever eventuality may occur in your marriage and, indeed, in your life long before you marry and certainly long before you find yourself in the midst of a divorce or dissolution of your marriage. Don't wait until the first signs of deterioration of your relationship to think about the possibility that you will be on your own without the comfort and security of a lifelong partner. It was but one generation back that women married young, raised families, provided a home for their working spouses, and did volunteer work. Times have changed, and whether it is for better or worse, the job market has opened to women. Over 50 percent of the workforce now is composed of women; the stay-at-home wife and mother appears to be the exception now.

With the opening of opportunities for women in the workplace have come responsibilities that are not always welcome. With this change in our social and family structure we have experienced a phenomenon: Women, including single parents with small children, are expected to work and to support themselves. Who wouldn't want to be able to do that? Unfortunately, the pay scale for women continues to lag far behind that of men in the majority of middle-income jobs.

Your challenge is to plan ahead for making your own way in the world. You may be a high school graduate, a college graduate, or neither. But it is you to whom you must look for your own support and satisfaction in life. Gone are the days when a young woman went from her father's home to her husband's home and there lived happily ever after. This fantasy dooms a young woman to victimization in love and in life.

The traditional view that marriage will provide economic security and support for life is unique to the American view of marriage. Our thesis is that security comes from the knowledge that, notwithstanding your marital status, you and you alone are capable of supporting yourself without reliance on the largesse of another or on an order of court that may be disobeyed before the ink is dry on the paper. We are not recommending that each bride delay her wedding until she has a Ph.D. Preparation begins early in the life of a girl and should be part of your preparation for your own daughter. A girl should begin in high school by setting academic goals and doing her best to achieve them. She should never be afraid to follow the different path or create her own style. The development of a woman's self-confidence begins early on and should be nourished and cherished by her. She should take the classes that are less traditional for girls. She should prepare herself.

Women and men are delaying their entry into marriage these days. Use that extra time between the end of your formal education and your marriage to establish yourself. While it is difficult to start out in the workplace at any time, it is easier to begin at age twenty or twenty-one than at age forty-five or fifty. Begin your career with a purpose and do not allow yourself to make your career secondary to your search for a husband.

Those women in their fifties and sixties who go through a divorce are those most damaged by the women's liberation movement, because their cultural upbringing did not prepare them to be self-supporting. This generation of women and prior generations were raised to marry, raise children, and provide a supportive home for their working spouses. Often they suffer the ignominy of a single life with little or no support from a spouse of many years, and nothing that they are qualified to do or prepared to learn to do to support themselves. It is a shock when these women find how ill prepared they are for life on their own. This is a situation you must work to avoid. And avoidance will come naturally if you are prepared. That is not to say that you are not justified in looking forward to marriage, children, and life with a loving husband. Those goals have not changed despite the professional demands placed on women. But those goals can be met in a more leisurely manner with some attention paid to the ultimate goal—that of taking care of yourself and knowing that no matter what happens, you will always be able to take care of yourself.

One way that you will take care of yourself is to consider the signing of a prenuptial agreement. In most other countries of the world, marriage is regarded in a more pragmatic way as a relationship between two people designed to fulfill mutual needs. A marriage contract signed before the consummation of the marriage is common in Europe, Latin America, Asia, and Africa. Yet the romantic ideal in America is that marriage is forever, and that to insist upon the signing of a premarital agreement is bad luck or displays a lack of commitment, faith, or love.

The American public has regarded with distaste rich men who require their prospective brides to sign premarital agreements, as did Ari Onassis of Jackie and Donald Trump of Ivana. In the past, premarital or prenuptial agreements were the province of the older, wealthy man marrying the sweet young penniless thing and his desire to protect his property from her demands in the event of divorce. Such agreements were not favored by the courts, which often found that the less wealthy (and usually less sophisticated) spouse was induced to sign the agreement through various devices, including undue influence, duress, or threats of refusal to go through with the wedding, which in most cases was scheduled for the day the agreement was presented to the bride for her signature.

Premarital agreements have come a long way. Because couples are marrying later, each may have had an opportunity to accumulate property prior to marriage, which they each may want to remain their separate property after marriage. A premarital agreement can accomplish that.

The attitude of the courts with regard to the enforcement of such agreements has changed. The Uniform Premarital Agreement Law has been adopted in all fifty states, indicating the acceptance of the concept. And judges now will examine the circumstances of execution of the agreement: Is it on the day of the wedding with the guests in the chapel or some two or more weeks before? Is the nonwealthy spouse represented by counsel? Does the agreement fairly state what property each has that they wish to maintain as separate as well as the value thereof? Still, courts will look at whether the terms of the agreement appear to be unconscionable. As people become more sophisticated and knowledgeable, their own responsibilities increase, and agreements that meet the test of the Uniform Premarital Agreement Law are now being upheld with great regularity.

Family Law in the Fifty States— Prenuptial Agreements*

View of Recent Cases in Various States

- ALABAMA
  The Cogginses entered into a prenuptial agreement saying that neither would ever file for a divorce, but that, if either of them did file for divorce, that spouse would pay the other from $1,000 to $5,000 a week in damages. The court threw out the agreement, saying it was unreasonable.

- NEVADA
  The Fickses signed a premarital agreement under which the bride-to-be waived any future alimony. The court ruled on appeal that the alimony waiver was no good because engaged couples have a confidential, fiduciary relationship, and the groom-to-be should have told her about his financial condition before she signed the agreement.

- FLORIDA
  The Osbornes had a prenuptial agreement saying the wife waived all rights to any property owned by the husband. The court awarded the home to the wife, but the appellate court reversed that, saying she was entitled to nothing, just as she had agreed in the prenuptial agreement.

  * Interpretations of the law vary from state to state and from time to time. These views are only illustrations, and you should check with current rulings in your own state.

A premarital agreement can be a means of protection for a non-wealthy and nonworking spouse, too. After all, you don't have to sign the agreement. And if you do, you should not have to give up your rights to accumulate community or joint property. You should bargain for a clause that provides for the creation of community property, despite the fact that your spouse intends to work at his separate business and maintain it as separate during the marriage. If it is unrealistic to expect that there will ever be any community property, you should bargain for a lump sum payment for each of the years of the marriage in the event of divorce. You should include within your premarital agreement obligations to provide for you in the event of your wealthy husband's death during the marriage. And you should certainly provide for a reexamination of the agreement in the event of the birth of children.

The Uniform Premarital Agreement Law as adopted by most states allows for an agreement prior to marriage on the amount and duration of support in the event of divorce. In some jurisdictions an agreement limiting support on divorce is considered against public policy because it is thought to promote divorce. Therefore, in such jurisdictions such a clause in the agreement is invalid. Usually, however, such an offensive clause can be severed from the balance of the agreement in the event of divorce. And a clever lawyer can draft an agreement that poses a certain term and amount of support as an attractive alternative to seeking support from a court on divorce.

Prior to your wedding, discuss with a family law attorney the meaning of the premarital agreement and fashion it to meet your needs. Do not be surprised if your prospective mate asks you to sign a premarital agreement. Just be prepared.

There are other, not so obvious advantages to a premarital agreement. It will force you and your fiancé to sit down together and discuss what your life and marriage goals are. The two of you will have an opportunity to develop a clear understanding of who the other is and what each of you expects from the marriage. You may find in these discussions that your expectations are so different that the marriage is doomed to fail. Pay heed to these warnings as they arise.

After the wedding you must continue to remain independent and knowledgeable. You are the one who should be in charge of the family finances even though you are staying home with the children. Don't for a minute think you don't have time to do this. Do it.

Family Law in the Fifty States—
More Prenuptial Agreements*

View of Recent Cases in Various States

- NEVADA
  In the case of *Sogg v. Nevada State Bank,* the court disallowed the prenuptial agreement because the husband did not reveal his net worth to his wife.

- TEXAS
  In *Winger v. Pianka,* an engaged couple signed a prenuptial agreement providing that each spouse's income after marriage would be that spouse's sole and separate property. The court upheld the agreement on appeal.

- WISCONSIN
  The court of appeals underscored that prenuptial agreements must contain a full disclosure of both parties' assets. It is not enough that reference be made to other documents or information—a financial statement of both parties must be part of the prenuptial agreement.

- WASHINGTON STATE
  It is all right, said the court in the Foran case, for a person to sign a financially unfair and one-sided prenuptial agreement, but only if the person fully understood how unfair the contract was.

Interpretations of the law vary from state to state and from time to time. These views are only illustrations, and you should check with current rulings in your own state.

Family Law in the Fifty States—
Cohabitation Agreements*

View of Recent Cases in Various States

- NORTH DAKOTA
  In *Kohler v. Flynn,* the court ruled that live-ins are not required to share their property with each other unless they have an agreement in writing.

- NEVADA
  The Nevada courts in *Western States Construction v. Michoff* ruled that a couple living together for nine years established a contract for equal division of property.

- GEORGIA
  Crooke and Gilden were lesbian lovers who had an agreement to live together, but when they had a fight and Crooke tried to sue Gilden under the contract, the trial court said the contract was illegal because the consideration for making the contract was an illegal and immoral relationship. The Supreme Court overturned that trial court ruling, saying that nothing in the cohabitation contract required either party to do anything illegal.

  *Interpretations of the law vary from state to state and from time to time. These views are only illustrations, and you should check with current rulings in your own state.

In most instances a hardworking spouse will be grateful for your interest and welcome your work on family finances. Be involved from the beginning. If you have not been involved, you will be at the mercy of others who may not know you or your husband nor your financial picture.

If your husband will not allow your participation—which in itself is a bad sign—do what you can with your own finances. Maintain accurate accounts so you can show what the lifestyle of the family is during the time of marriage in the event that you are confronted with divorce. Maintain your own financial independence. Keep your own assets separate. Do not put your husband's name on your separate real property just because some lending institution says you must. If you are compelled to do so, obtain a quit-claim deed concurrently with the execution of the grant deed. Always maintain your separate charge accounts so you have credit in the event of divorce.

Avoid signing on to such myths of marriage as the Cinderella myth, that is, that being married will relieve the frustration, pain, and struggle in your life. The truth is that life is always full of problems and marriage brings its own set, including those of your new spouse.

The Cinderella myth lulls a woman into thinking that love and marriage is forever (and we hope it is), and that she never need trouble herself about family finances, her husband's business, or keeping understandable financial records. This is a dangerous attitude, and if divorce occurs—as it does in almost 50 percent of marriages—the ignorant spouse is at a terrific disadvantage.

Knowledge is power—this concept, central to winning in war, is a maxim equally applicable to the war of divorce. Know the financial facts of your marriage. Do not allow yourself to be the victim in divorce.

Your idyllic marriage will change from the day you say "I do." The relationship between spouses never remains the same as on the wedding day. Even if there is never a divorce, people change and grow. Be sure you are growing with the marriage.

CHAPTER THREE

What to Do When Your Marriage Is Dying

THIS CHAPTER WILL:

> I. Help you know if your marriage is in trouble
> II. Outline your alternatives if it is in trouble
> III. Show you how to protect yourself

I. HOW TO TELL IF YOUR MARRIAGE IS IN TROUBLE

If love is blind, that blindness sometimes carries over into marriage. The curious thing about many divorces is that often the spouses miss or ignore the telltale signs. To the unwary wife or husband, the divorce sometimes comes like a bolt of lightning out of the blue. Yet to outsiders the coming divorce is often very obvious.

It is interesting that most divorces occur for the same reason that most marriages occur. Most women, according to contemporary studies, marry for the emotional connection between themselves and the men in their lives. When they think they have made an emotional connection with an acceptable man, women tend to marry. When they find that the emotional connection is broken, most women divorce. Obviously, we each marry for various and different reasons, including security, desire for children, and pressures from our peers or family. Still, most surveys confirm that women are more likely to marry for love and emotional stability, and when they are in a marriage that doesn't provide those, or when marriage becomes a lonely life of isolation and abuse from the partner or a combination of both, divorce becomes a serious option.

A. Two Myths About Marriage and Divorce

There are two great myths about marriage and divorce that, unfortunately, make too many of us ashamed that we failed at marriage and guilty because we think it was our fault.

The first myth is that it wasn't like this in the "olden days," when our grandparents married for life and divorce was unthinkable. While it is true that earlier generations stigmatized divorce, sociologist William J. Goode, formerly on the faculty of Stanford and Harvard universities, says the perception of grandparents' marriages being better than our own is classic nostalgia for the perceived easier and simpler times of the past. In our view, that notion happens to be quite wrong or, at least, inconclusive. Marriages were just as unhappy in those "olden days" as they are now, but people could not divorce easily and remained trapped in their misery. There is no more sense in doing that today than there is in refusing the modern medical treatment that was not available to our grandparents.

We need to remember that life expectancy, significantly shorter in days gone by, has, astonishingly, almost doubled in this century. In previous centuries most people didn't live beyond what we now consider to be middle age. This was so true that, for example, menopause was not a major event in most women's lives because they never became old enough to reach that stage. In days gone by, people married and had children, and by the time the children were grown and off to school, the husband and wife had but a few years left to live; divorce, therefore, was impractical.

The second myth is that the high divorce rate—roughly one out of two marriages ends in divorce—is something peculiar to the United States. Dr. Goode makes the point that there is a high divorce rate in almost all industrialized countries. This may be because women are less dependent on men for financial security in such countries and economically more able to support themselves outside of marriage. Modern times have brought a liberalization of sexual mores and greater opportunities for women to live on their own without suffering the "old maid" label.

In Dr. Goode's study of more than thirty countries, he notes a significant rise in divorce among all industrialized countries, including those with strong Catholic traditions such as Italy, France, and Spain. Goode believes that we need to recognize that divorce is a natural part of our culture and social life and adjust to it to make it less painful.

As a mark of our changing social culture, one woman comedian says that the first question she asks when she starts dating a man is whether he is the kind of person she wants her children to visit on weekends.

The causes of severance of the loving link between husband and wife run the gamut. Modern times have brought new sources of friction and distress between spouses, including a husband's resentment of his wife's successful career with concomitant freedom to do nontraditional things with her life. The economic recession has exacerbated the pressures on marriages; many companies are "downsizing" and laying off longtime workers, middle-aged and middle-class men who have always had a job and supported themselves and their families. These men are not just being laid off by IBM, AT&T, Xerox, and Bank of America; their jobs are permanently gone. If the husband has had a long career providing financial security and stature, and suddenly all that disappears, so does his self-esteem. Often the male response to such a situation is to withdraw into drug or alcohol abuse, distance himself from his wife through emotional and physical abuse, absent himself from the home, or remain in the house engrossed in himself, with the silences between him and other family members becoming long and frequent. Substance abuse is a major contributor to divorce, but it is only a symptom of the deeper alienation, resentment, and fear spouses have developed and which they refuse to or cannot work through together.

A keen barometer of a marriage in trouble is sex or lack thereof. In one survey 72 percent of women reported that sexual incompatibility was an important cause of their divorces. Among younger women, there was a tendency to lose interest sexually in the husband first, while among older women the reverse tended to be true. The loss of sexual compatibility ranges from mismatched desires to frequency and type of sex. The loss of this emotional connection often leads to alienation and withdrawal, to loss of passion, and possibly to infidelity. A note on the modern marriage is that, among the higher income brackets, more wives seek refuge in extramarital affairs than do women in lower income brackets.

Another fascinating aspect of divorce (and marriage) is that many women know they are in the wrong marriage very early in the game. In one survey, 54 percent of divorced women said they knew it wasn't going to work from the first year. However, and this is a critical point for us to understand, although a wife may know a marriage is in trouble, most women move slowly to do something about it. The average woman in this circumstance does not act until the marriage is four years old. And the average separation lasts up to two years before divorce is finally initiated.

B. Pre-Wedding Myths About Marriage

There are other well-known myths that serve to undermine the marriage, even before the wedding. According to Jacqueline Cook, marriage and family therapist at the University of Oklahoma, two other great myths exist about marriage *before* the wedding that often lead to divorce after marriage:

The first is that the other person can be changed or molded significantly to make him or her into the perfect spouse. Men and women are constantly surprised, says Cook, "that they are unable to change their spouse's 'undesirable' habits after marriage. People still enter marriage believing that any annoying habit or patterns their partners have will disappear after the marriage or that they can mold their partners to fit their own designs." A variation of this is that you will become accustomed to those habits of your partner that you don't like and they will no longer be an issue. Just the opposite is true. Those little annoying traits become major irritants.

The second myth, according to Cook, is that the birth of a child will bring the parents together and rescue a foundering marriage. This also is rarely accurate, and when the unreality of these two myths comes home to the married couple, says Cook, divorce looks like the only option. "In American society today, there is a definite quick-fix, 'fast food' type focus."

C. Telltale Signs Your Marriage Is in Trouble

Here are some of the telltale signs that your marriage is in trouble and may be headed for divorce:

1. *You're roommates and not a couple.* Are you living with someone and still lonely? Is your life basically just like the one you lived at school or at home with your sister? Both of you are living separate lives with the same family name and address, but you are not an intimate couple. The shared moments of shared spirits aren't there. You are alone together. You talk easily about who will pick up the dry cleaning and what is needed from the store, but you have stopped talking about dreams, hopes, and fears for the future.

Clues that something is wrong: if telephone conversations shift to another subject when you enter the room; if mail disappears; if credit card bills are snatched away, preventing your seeing the details of all the charges; if there are unfamiliar telephone numbers on your phone bill; if there is a significant change in behavior patterns, such as more late evenings at the office and more business trips.

2. *Sex is a stranger to your bed.* It's an old wives' tale that if the sex is good, the marriage is good. Old wives or not, sex *is* an excellent barometer of weather on the marriage front. Good sex, engaged in eagerly and pleasurably by both partners, defines an intimacy that bonds the couple as a couple. Perfunctory, routine sex with one partner participating because it is expected is the sign of stormy weather for a marriage.

3. *You're openly hostile.* Has open hostility surfaced in your relationship? Are you nagging at each other, blaming each other, feeling sorry for yourself because you feel you are carrying the burdens of your partner and he is not responsive to your burdens? When one of you seeks advice, comfort, or solace from your spouse, does your

mate act as if it is an imposition to deal with or that your problem is *your* fault instead of a joint issue that the two of you will work together to solve? Are there accusations and arguments over seemingly trivial issues? Very often at this stage of the marriage there are fights over little things, which are really fights over much larger issues that are never mentioned.

Are you flooded by your partner's emotions? Does he get angry or agitated about something and do you find yourself saying to yourself, "I hate this! I don't need this! I've got to get out of here!"? This is a sure warning sign your marriage is in trouble.

4. *You're AWOL from each other*. Is each of you turning more and more away from the other? Is his golf or video game more important than sharing time with you? Is your volunteer activity and shopping more important than spending time with him? Are outside recreations, extra workloads, trips, meetings, conventions, night classes, and other diversions cutting down on the time you have available to spend with each other? In other words, when you're together do either of you think of four other places you'd rather be?

5. *You're involved in "sports" sex*. By the time you have gotten to being away more and more from each other, you have also probably gotten to being more and more with someone else who provides what is missing from your marriage, namely, sex, intimacy, sharing, and emotional release (without the responsibilities of marriage, of course). In short, you have stopped playing house with the one you're married to and started playing love tryst with someone else. Either you or your mate may be involved in an extramarital affair; the result is the same. The marriage is in trouble.

Another measure of the stability of your marriage is suggested by a recent study on this engaging subject by Dr. John Gottman of the University of Washington. The Gottman group has evolved an eleven-question test that it claims can predict which marriages will survive and which will end in divorce. These eleven questions deal with how the couples met, wooed, and married and about the good times and bad times and their philosophy of their marriages. Applied to some fifty-six couples who cooperated with the study by talking with Gottman's group while being videotaped and connected to a polygraph, it has had a 94% accuracy.

The Gottman team predicted that ten of the fifty-six couples would be divorced within three years, and sure enough, according to a report in the *Journal of Family Psychology,* seven of the couples were divorced at the end of the three years.

According to the Gottman studies, the indications of trouble in a marriage can be spotted years before the specter of divorce becomes real. Perhaps the most surprising conclusion of the Gottman studies is that the one most dependable sign of marital trouble is the husband's disappointment with the marriage—not the wife's.

Some of the other clues concern the way the couple views its relationship; if they are disappointed in marriage; if they display affection openly toward each other; and their memories of their courtship and marriage.

Dr. Gottman says that there is what he calls "a cascade toward divorce," marked by five traits. The first is the tidal wave of a partner's negative feelings, where your marriage partner seems angry about everything. Second, these couples see the problems of their marriage as oppressive and probably beyond solution. Third, a corollary to the second is that they don't see any point in working out their problems—the problems are too extreme and the marriage isn't worth enough to try saving it. Fourth, they begin living in parallel; they don't share meals or free time and develop a set of friends apart from each other. Finally, while they are married, they are terribly lonely.

According to Gottman, the cascade toward divorce begins internally within each partner and then finally surfaces in two hurtful ways. The first is outgoing, as one partner engages in ridicule and reproach of his or her spouse, and the second is becoming defensive and pulling oneself into one's own fortress of silence.

6. *You're saying the D-word out loud.* Are the two of you saying the Big D-word—DIVORCE—aloud to each other? This is usually not only a sure sign that your marriage is in trouble, but that it is in terminal condition because each of you has been saying the D-word to him- or herself secretly for some time. By this time, you have also been saying the D-word aloud to close friends and other members of the family, but your spouse is usually the last one to whom you will say it. By that time you will have progressed fairly far along toward your decision before the word comes out of your mouth.

Somewhere during this process you are actually going to say the D-word secretly to yourself: DIVORCE. Mark that moment because it is important in the scheme of protecting yourself and coming out a winner. Mark it well. When you conclude that the marriage is nearly dead and all that remains are the funeral arrangements, you should immediately move to protect yourself, to position yourself to emerge a winner in the event the word DIVORCE moves you into court.

II. WHAT ARE YOUR ALTERNATIVES?

When you finally decide that your marriage is dead, you have two basic alternatives: Stay or leave.

A. Stay

There are many reasons you may decide to stay in the marriage; the most common reasons are:

1. *Money*. You are afraid that you will be forced into a less secure and less comfortable lifestyle. In fact, that is usually more often true than not. The standard of living for women tends to drop after a divorce. The reasons: There is not enough to go around upon divorce to support two homes, and the newly divorced woman has not prepared herself for the reality of life, that she must rely on herself to provide her own life style; she may not have received a fair settlement with which she can be comfortable. This book is dedicated to assisting you if you do go through a divorce.

2. *Loneliness*. It isn't pleasant for people to be alone; most would rather have some company than no company at all. Some of us are unable to be content alone with ourselves. In fact, the problem may be that you are not comfortable with yourself and you require the validation of a man to prove that you are worthy. How many women do you know who need to validate themselves through a man; who need to prove they are attractive enough to snag a husband? With these women, the problem is their image of themselves. Divorce will not resolve this lack of confidence.

3. *Children*. Worrying about how the divorce will affect the children is a major reason that women stay in a marriage; often women are willing to endure severe hardship to hold the household together for the sake of the children. However, the presence of children is all the more reason for assuring your financial security and theirs.

4. *Hope*. Some women cling to the hope that the marriage will ultimately work out because they still love their husbands (or think

they do) and hope he will change into a different man who will make their marriage work. Too often this is hope over reality. It is truly a source of bewilderment as to why women marry and stay with men who are different from the sort of men they wanted to marry.

5. *Pregnancy*. If you become pregnant, of course, you feel more vulnerable. The problems of financial security and loneliness are even more difficult to face. That does not mean that divorce is not an alternative.

6. *Outside pressure*. Sometimes there is no internal glue holding the marriage together, but only pressure from outside from family, friends, or church to hold the marriage together.

7. *Frustration and fear*. Another reason women stay in an unhappy marriage is that they fear starting over again with the dating game and courting with a different man. Or they may enjoy some aspects of marriage (sex or stature in the community or lifestyle) and are reluctant to give them up.

Given all these reasons for staying in an unhappy marriage, it is interesting to note that the greatest single regret harbored by most divorced women is that they didn't divorce sooner. Divorce opened a door to new freedom and confidence and, usually, new and better relationships.

If you do stay in your dormant marriage, you are certain to have to cope with emotional problems. How one personally copes with the situation depends on one's own emotional stability and will vary with everyone's personality. Whether you live separate lives and endure the time you have together while ignoring the time you are apart, or live in an armed camp with constant conflict, is primarily an emotional choice. However, there may be economic consequences of your decision to lead separate lives. If you continue to be legally married, but emotionally divorced, both of you are entitled to share the combined income and assets of the marriage. You should act to protect yourself legally to make sure your husband isn't hiding income or assets from you, for he may be preparing for what he sees as the ultimate eventuality: divorce. If you are actually separated, in some jurisdictions the wage earner's salary is separate property. You should check with an attorney familiar with the law in your geographical area to protect your rights.

B. Leave

If you decide to leave the relationship, there are several alternatives, including simply walking out, annulment, a legal separation, and divorce. Most of our attention will be on obtaining a divorce because that is the most common choice. However, there are legal consequences arising from each of the other alternatives.

1. *Walking out*. Sometimes just walking out the door and not turning back seems appealing. It is neat. It is clean. It is quick. It is also stupid and may carry adverse consequences to you. Even so, enough people do it for it to be mentioned here.

In some jurisdictions you will be viewed as deserting the marriage, which puts you in a weak position under the law. You are viewed as having abandoned the marriage, and in the process abandoned all legal claims to your property and other legal rights. The law varies from state to state, but to prove abandonment a period of time is required before the law considers the marriage dissolved. This can vary from a few months to a number of years. The legal effect of your walking out of a marriage should be understood and carefully considered before you take that route.

2. *Annulment*. Annulment generally means that the marriage never legally existed, and in some states there may be nothing to settle. Most states have a set of circumstances under which an annulment will be granted. The usual causes are

- marriage of blood relatives of close degree
- bigamy
- insanity
- legal incapacity [usually, too young]
- duress
- fraud
- concealed felony conviction or addiction or pregnancy
- impotency

Annulment is like a divorce in that you petition the court to set aside the marriage as if it never happened. However, assets acquired during a marriage that is annulled will be equitably divided.

3. *Separation*. Legal separation is a divorce from the bed and board of your spouse and involves separate households and separate maintenance. If done properly with a written agreement, the court

divides property and orders support, but the couple legally remains married. Spouses opt for a legal separation instead of divorce for a variety of reasons including religious affiliation or tax advantages. Senior citizens sometimes do so for financial security to take advantage of social security or a pension. Sometimes it is done as a prelude to divorce or to make the steps toward the ultimate divorce easier. We're told that television talk-show host Tom Snyder and his wife were legally separated for years to protect financial interests they owned jointly.

So, legal separation is common when you and your husband want to maintain some of the advantages of the marriage without having to share the same bed. There are other reasons for a legal separation, such as social stature or money, but the separation contract must clearly spell out the rights and obligations between the two of you to assure your protection and fair treatment. Legal separation also carries hazards of which you must be aware to protect yourself from the irresponsible behavior of your husband. For example, you want to have agreements restraining his squandering the marital property, half of which under most circumstances is yours. Using your half of the property of the marriage to entertain and support an extramarital relationship is not a recommended method of protecting your property.

Advantages of Legal Separation

- It provides a cooling-off period during which both parties have a chance to think over what they are doing and, possibly, to reconcile.
- It helps husband and wife to move into the mental and emotional mind-set of being apart and, possibly, divorced. It may ease the parties into the final resolution of their relationship.
- The legal and economic benefits of being married continue, such as health insurance, pensions, inheritance, and a stronger credit rating.
- It is usually quicker and easier to obtain an order for a legal separation than a divorce. Such benefits of a divorce as separate homes and freedom from the strain of an unhappy relationship are realized much more quickly. If both parties

want a legal separation, it is easier to obtain in those jurisdictions where it is necessary to meet residence requirements to file for divorce.

Disadvantages of Separation

- If the marriage is doomed, it is possible that the separation
  will simply prolong the process, which, in turn, may make it
  that much more painful. Depending on the law in your
  state, it could also be financially more expensive if you go on
  to obtain a divorce later because there may be some duplica-
  tion of attorney fees and court costs.
- It sometimes gives the edge to the husband with the job
  because the nonworking wife will not have the economic
  benefits of living together.
- Because you are still technically married, you might be held
  responsible for the debts or actions of your husband. The
  separation agreement can protect against that, but if a third-
  party creditor sues you, claiming you are responsible for
  your husband's credit card debts, you will have the expense
  of defending yourself. Also, you and your husband may still
  be treated as a married couple for purposes of pensions, life
  insurance, and other contractual obligations. In order to
  avoid much of this hassle, you need a carefully drawn separation agreement that is approved by the court. If you reach
  this point, it is a simple matter to change the legal separation to a divorce when the time comes, as it almost always
  does.

4. *Divorce.* Divorce is the ultimate demise of the marriage to
which desertion and separation usually lead. In this book divorce is
our main focus because it is, unfortunately, the most frequently chosen alternative. It is complicated—complicated because people are
complicated. Usually, divorcing couples are as consumed by the emotions of the divorce as they were when they married and were consumed by the emotions of the marriage. What's missing in most
divorces is the love and mutual respect once cherished by the parties.
Somebody once correctly said that marriage is about love and divorce
is about money. We believe that's quite accurate.

When you decide to move ahead with a divorce, you should be as confident as you can that you understand what is ahead for you. In fact, you probably should give your divorce more thought than you gave your wedding. For a fast reality check, understand that divorce is

- a *big* decision
- an *expensive* process
- an *emotional* roller coaster

and that you will have fewer assets than you share with your husband, and your standard of living will probably be lower than that which you enjoyed together.

Given that divorce is often better than the hell you are living in, if you go ahead, your twin objectives should be to obtain the best property settlement possible in an expeditious and amicable manner so you can begin your new life as soon as reasonably possible.

III. HOW YOU CAN PROTECT YOURSELF

Once you have decided it's over, the business of protecting yourself is just beginning. (Let's hope you have begun the job of protecting yourself before that by making positive life decisions.) Here we discuss how you can protect yourself mentally, emotionally, and legally so you come out a winner and not a basket case.

Your single most important goal is protection for yourself. You may have to protect yourself physically from an abusive husband; you will have to protect yourself emotionally because uncoupling the relationship will be traumatic; and you definitely will have to protect yourself financially to ensure that what you take away from the marriage is your fair share.

A. Your Mental Preparation

Here are some facts to have clear in your head so you can protect yourself mentally and emotionally in the divorce:

1. *Your lawyer can't and won't do it all*. Don't be a passive spectator at your own divorce. You weren't a passive spectator at your own wedding, and your divorce is much more important and more com-

plicated. It's the marriage whose funeral you are attending—not yours. Your life is ahead, and your ability to take control of the divorce process will substantially enhance your life ahead.

2. *Don't wallow in the pain of your dead marriage*. You have a life to live ahead of you. You will find new serenity and happiness. Meantime, it will not help to whine—not even to yourself—about the hurt, the sacrifice, and the injustice. Just do what you have to do and move on.

3. *You shouldn't play lawyer*. Discuss your course of action with your lawyer. Don't make any major moves without checking with her; certainly, moving out of the family residence and agreeing to financial arrangements are critical decisions you need to understand from the legal perspective before you act. Leaving home, for example, might jeopardize your rights to custody of the children.

4. *He is not your husband anymore—he's your adversary*. Don't assume your husband will take care of you. For example, upon separation you and your attorney will try to obtain an agreement with your husband for generous temporary support. Voluntary temporary payments from your husband may set a precedent for the amount the final support or alimony award will be. Remember, the assets of the marriage that were acquired after you got married—excluding usually inheritances or gifts—are yours, too. Don't be hesitant about seizing assets to help you support yourself.

5. *You should socialize carefully*. Don't date during a period of temporary separation. You don't want the appearance of extramarital relationships to cloud your rights to child custody or in some jurisdictions to your one-half of the assets. Don't have sex with your husband during a separation—not a good idea. In some states, it could nullify any legal waiting period. Go easy on the development of other relationships. Having another man around may be a comfort, but it could be a disservice to you because such relationships during negotiations tend to muddy the water.

6. *Be prepared to protect yourself physically*. If your husband becomes a physical threat or stalks you, immediately call the police; get "stay away" orders through the court; make him post a peace bond; and take self-protective measures. This is very serious business, and you must treat it as such.

7. *Act like a savvy adult with your husband*. While you need not be overly loving to your future ex, you should always be polite—not

docile—and avoid arguing and fighting during separation. Assume your spouse will hate your lawyer and say nasty things about her. Ignore the insults. And, most important of all, rehearse saying over and over, "Your lawyer should talk to my lawyer about that."

B. Understanding the Enemy

First, understand that if your husband is planning on a divorce, he has probably already initiated a divorce strategy to ensure that he has the advantage. Whether you realize it or not, at this point you are living with the enemy, someone who is determined to destroy the marriage and take what he can for himself. To get out of this comfortably, you have to fight back. You must be in charge initially; find out what is happening; protect yourself by being aware of or becoming aware of what your assets are and where they are.

The strategy adopted by most husbands is to dominate, control, and perhaps obscure all information that can hurt him and to gain control of the marital property. This means, for example, he will try to keep any information about what he is doing out of your reach. He will try to keep compromising mail from coming home, limit phone calls to your home, and bring nothing home in his pockets, wallet, briefcase, or the car (of course, he will *always* make a mistake and bring something home that will arouse your suspicions).

To maintain control of the joint property, he may refuse to move out of the house and urge you to move instead. He may bleed bank accounts, take physical possession of stocks, bonds, insurance policies, coin or stamp collections, rare books or artifacts, and financial records. He may squirrel away cash in a separate account and close out joint charge accounts or max them out so you can't use them. He may eat out frequently, buy more expensive clothes, and run up car expenses, all to establish the business expenses that he believes will reduce the joint income you are to share and possibly the value of the business. He may report to credit card companies that he lost his wallet, with the result that existing cards are canceled. Then he will have replacement cards sent to him at another address. He may urge you to go to work or take a second job to increase your own level of income so you will have a smaller claim on his.

His first and last objectives may be to secure as much of the joint property, money, and credit lines from you and attempt to establish your minimal need for support.

The clever husband planning on divorce will accomplish this secretly, before the divorce process is officially begun. However, if you are alert, you will plan strategically yourself and beat him to it.

C. Your Husband's Game Plan

Consider the kind of advice your husband's attorney is giving him. Following is from a list of don'ts given to husbands by their own divorce attorneys, who are charged with securing the best settlement for their clients. If you understand what your husband is trying to accomplish, it can strengthen your resolve to do what you have to do and to avoid some of the common traps of the dissolution process.

- Don't sign an agreement.
- Don't verbally agree to anything.
- Don't talk to your wife's lawyer.
- Don't move out of the family residence—yet.
- Don't start paying support on a regular basis—yet.
- Don't say, "It's all right with me if you leave."
- Don't fight in front of the kids.
- Don't abuse your wife or threaten her.
- Don't feel bad about yourself.
- Don't feel she's the only woman in the world.
- Don't turn to drink or drugs.
- Don't become a swinger.
- Don't hang around people who blame you.
- Don't hang around others in the same spot you are.
- Don't feel guilty.
- Don't think she or her lawyer will be reasonable.

As you can see, this is good advice for you, too.

D. At the End

Marriage is two people merging their lives, their fortunes, and their future. Divorce is the uncoupling of all that.

In this chapter we have tried to help you recognize

1. If your marriage is in trouble, and if so, is separation or divorce a possibility;
2. What your alternatives are: stay or leave;
3. How to protect yourself in the process of separation or divorce.

CHAPTER FOUR

Choosing a Lawyer: Your Most Important Decision

THIS CHAPTER WILL HELP YOU:

I. Find a divorce attorney
II. Choose the best attorney for you and your divorce
III. Handle the preliminary attorney interview
IV. Avoid common pitfalls and mistakes
V. Understand what your lawyer will and will not do for you
VI. Give you ten important points to remember

I. HOW TO FIND A DIVORCE ATTORNEY

Choosing a good attorney to represent you in divorce is the most important decision you will make after you have determined to divorce your husband.

What you are looking for is a lawyer who combines firmness, experience, and knowledge of the law—a skilled negotiator and confessional priest. You need a combination of Clint Eastwood, Henry Kissinger, and Mother Teresa.

The legal profession is just like baseball or lion taming. There are good players and tamers and there are poor players and tamers. Poor baseball players tend to lose and poor lion tamers tend to get eaten alive. Your choice of a divorce lawyer could mean the difference between winning and being eaten alive.

Understand clearly at the beginning that the wife is very often at a disadvantage in a divorce proceeding: financially, emotionally, mentally, and socially.

Of course, you may think about not getting a lawyer at all. This is invariably a bad decision. You wouldn't try to do your own dental work, so why would you place legal, financial, and personal problems as significant and complicated as your divorce in the hands of an amateur—namely you, or worse yet, you and your about-to-be ex-husband?

This is not to say that there aren't some times when you can handle your divorce yourself. Those are the marriages of less than six months to a year, without children, and without significant assets, *and* when you are able to support yourself. Otherwise, you ought to have professional representation.

A. Finding a Good Lawyer

This is not as complicated as it may seem, but it takes time. You should shop for a divorce lawyer in the same way you shop for a dentist or doctor.

1. *Referral by friends or relatives.* One of the most common ways of finding any professional is by references from other people. If you have worked successfully with a lawyer on other matters but she is not a divorce lawyer, ask for a referral to a divorce specialist.

Ask friends or relatives who have been divorced for their recommendations. Ask religious counselors, family counselors, therapists, and even business associates. However, do not rely on any of these recommendations in and of themselves. It is mandatory that you interview these lawyers yourself before you make your choice.

2. *Legal referral services.* The local bar association in the community where you live usually has a referral service listed in the telephone book. Or, you may contact the American Academy of Matri-monial Lawyers, 20 North Michigan Avenue, Chicago, Illinois

60602 ([312]263-6477) or the American Bar Association, 750 N. Lake Shore Drive, Chicago, Illinois 60611 ([312] 988-5520). Both these national organizations can refer you to attorneys specializing in divorce and family law near you. We have also listed a number of sources in each state in the appendix of this book.

3. *Advertising.* Attorneys are now ethically permitted to advertise, and that may be a source to consider. However, just as in the case of any other service, you must judge the attorney by her ability and not the effectiveness of her advertising. A lawyer's advertisement will be the least likely source of accurate information about the lawyer's level of expertise.

4. *Legal clinics and limited-cost alternatives.* There are low-cost law firms such as Jacoby & Meyers; lawyers who work with your credit union, labor union, or religious group; or even credit card companies. American Express, for example, now offers a legal services plan. There are also government-funded legal services such as city, county, and state legal clinics in some areas, as well as the Legal Aid Society, which has been in business in most sections of the United States for many years. In Los Angeles County, for example, the Harriet Buhai Center for Family Law helps people help themselves.

The shortcoming of many of these limited-cost alternatives and clinics is that the attorneys are overworked; in addition, some do not specialize in divorce, and therefore have limited experience in divorce and marital negotiation. Family or marital law is vastly different from most civil law in that it includes a superheated emotional aspect. Although divorce is technically about custody of money and dependents, there is a strong emotional undercurrent throughout the proceedings that general practice attorneys rarely know how to cope with. At the same time, there are complex issues of valuation of real property, taxes, and division of business assets that require experience and knowledge to work through.

5. *Classes and support groups.* Most communities have schools with courses in family relations. A member of the faculty might guide you to a competent family law attorney. In addition, there is a wide variety of support groups for women, abused spouses, seniors, and others where you may find direction to attorneys specializing in family law. Many of these are listed in the newspapers regularly and in most telephone directories under Support Groups, Community Groups, Legal Assistance, and Family Services. Many groups that are

operating in areas other than divorce involve or have contact with family law attorneys. Those include adoption and foster care agencies, alcohol and drug abuse centers, child abuse and family violence services, family counseling centers, family planning services, mental health and crisis intervention centers, and senior citizen and youth service centers.

In addition, there are such nonprofit organizations as Parents Without Partners; Alcoholics Anonymous; Cocaine Anonymous; National Institute on Drug Abuse; battered women's shelters; Parents Anonymous; National Association of Social Workers; Jewish Family Services; Catholic Family Services; neighborhood legal services; American Psychological Association; Catholic Charities; Batterers Anonymous; crisis resolution clinics; domestic abuse centers; Catholic Psychological Services; centers for family counseling; the social services organizations of many Protestant denominations; and Women Helping Women.

This array of nonprofit or government organizations that could help refer you to appropriate family law attorneys is generally listed in the yellow pages under the categories "Crisis Intervention Service," "Information Bureaus & Services," "Recorded Information," or "Social Service Organizations."

6. *Directories of attorneys.* At the public library, you can consult several excellent directories of attorneys that will tell you about particular lawyer's practices, their specialties, their education and background. These include Martindale-Hubbell, a giant reference work found at most major libraries. It lists lawyers all around the country as well as worldwide. The entries in Martindale are paid for by the lawyers who are listed, but these will be helpful in telling you the kinds of law each lawyer practices and her background. One thing worth looking for is whether or not the lawyer is a certified family law specialist.

There is another directory that is worthwhile, although it does not list as broad a range of attorneys and is focused on the states of Florida, New Jersey, New York, Massachusetts, New Hampshire, and Virginia. There is a separate book for each of those six states, and the prices vary from $35 to $55 as of mid-1994. The volumes are available directly from the publisher, Skinder-Strauss Associates, Newark, New Jersey (1-800-444-4041), and are called, collectively, the *Lawyers Diary and Manual.*

The American Academy of Matrimonial Lawyers has a directory of its members. It is a national organization and its members are generally tops in the family law field.

B. Individual Attorney or Full-Service Law Firm?

Part of your decision about whom to hire will include deciding whether you should be represented by an attorney working alone in her own practice or working with a full-service legal group. A full-service law firm may include lawyers with varying specialties, including tax and estate planning and litigation specialists. There are, of course, advantages and disadvantages to both, and you need to weigh these in terms of what is most appropriate and easiest for you during the difficult business of dissolving your marriage.

1. *Individual attorney*. The advantage of hiring a sole practitioner is that she will be the only lawyer handling your case; you will know your lawyer well and she will know you. The disadvantage is that the individual attorney may not have the range of experience to understand all the substantive legal aspects of your case even if that attorney specializes in family or marital law. Also, while some individual attorneys may be less expensive, she may demand immediate payment of fees and charges because she does not have the resources to carry clients without being paid.

The fact is that most sole practitioners of note are more expensive, demanding at least $25,000 up front to take the case. Of course, there are some who are less expensive. In either case, the size of the retainer does not guarantee competency.

The principal disadvantage to the use of a sole practitioner is that her time is generally stretched to the limit. After all, the lawyer puts food on her family's table by selling her time. However, most of the well-known sole practitioners in the field of family law are tops in their field because they *do* specialize. Whatever you do, don't hire a sole practitioner who does personal injury or any other kind of work in addition to family law. Such a lawyer may not have the range of experience to deal with all the complexities—tax, real property, bankruptcy—and evaluations required of the specialist in family law.

Finally, if the case unexpectedly becomes complicated or drawn out, the individual attorney may be stretched too thin to do a good job for you because your case requires more time and energy than originally anticipated.

2. *Full-service law firm.* Even in a full-service law firm, you must be sure that your case is being handled by a lawyer or lawyers who specialize in family law. There are a few law firms that have under one roof many attorneys specializing in family law. With such a firm, you want to make sure that you are getting an experienced family law practitioner and that the firm is not training its new associate on your dollar.

A full-service law firm will provide you, the client, with other specialists if needed. But you must demand that your personal lawyer devote herself to family law. Usually, the lawyer doing family law in a full-service firm is, indeed, a specialist and has the advantage of having tax or other specialists working with her. While you must insist that you be represented by one lawyer only, another advantage of a full-service firm is that it generally has associates who can do certain of the work required in your case at a much lower cost than the family law specialist who will be directing those associates.

Fees and costs for a larger law firm may be higher than that of a sole practitioner, but not always. This is a matter of the individual lawyers. In large metropolitan areas, it is not unheard of for sole practitioners to charge $450 an hour or more. Sometimes arrangements for payments can be more flexible because a larger law firm may be able to accommodate different payment plans. However, pressures to bill and collect are high in all law firms.

The advantage to you of the larger full-service firm is the array of talent and resources available and the possibility that the large, prestigious law firm may, because of its very size and power, intimidate opposing counsel to effect a more expeditious settlement of your divorce.

No matter what lawyer is recommended to you, make the choice personally, yourself. There are incompetent lawyers. There are incompatible lawyers. There are inexperienced lawyers. There are lawyers whose training and experience are too narrow to enable them to do a good job in a complicated case. Family law is a composite practice with elements of tax, estate planning, accounting, evaluation of business assets, and sometimes bankruptcy. The practitioner needs to be smart and experienced. It is not unusual for you to ask prospective lawyers for names of former clients to call for a reference. This underscores a critically important aspect of choosing your divorce attorney, namely, you must be compatible with that attorney.

II. CHOOSING THE BEST LAWYER FOR YOU AND YOUR DIVORCE

A. What a Good Lawyer Should Be

1. *Legally competent.* Your attorney will be handling three types of work for you during your divorce, and she must have the professional competence to handle all three. These three types of work are legal research and writing connected with the divorce; negotiations with the opposing side—which is how most cases are resolved even before going to court; and trying the case in court if it becomes impossible to settle through negotiation.

2. *Compatible.* Your attorney is not your therapist or your best friend, yet she will be helping you through one of the most unfamiliar and traumatic periods of your life. Your attorney must, therefore, be someone with whom you are comfortable in a crisis situation and who will know your most intimate and embarrassing secrets but still be discreet and sensitive to your particular situation. She will understand that this is a strange situation for you, and will help guide you though it and help you understand what is happening without taking advantage of your vulnerability or misleading you. Your lawyer needs to be able to listen to you.

3. *Financially competent.* Divorce, as we said before, is about money, and your attorney must be knowledgeable about finances. She needn't be an accountant or banker, but she must understand real estate, financial accounts, stocks and bonds, options, pensions, and, generally, the financial world. Lacking that, she should have a professional financial adviser readily available to be assured of the best representation for you. Many times your lawyer will suggest hiring a forensic accountant. That is not because your lawyer is a dummy but only because it takes a special expertise to understand the books and records of many closely owned businesses.

4. *Candid.* Your lawyer must tell you what she or he honestly thinks the divorce will cost; what the problems are; and what your advantages are. Many of the decisions with which you will be confronted during the course of divorce cannot—nor should they—be made by your attorney. You must make these decisions yourself, but your attorney can help you by setting out the legal and life consequences of the alternatives you have available to you. You and your

attorney must work together to help you reach decisions that are best for you in your individual situation.

B. What Your Lawyer Shouldn't Be

1. *In conflict with your interests.* You and your husband must not share one lawyer. A friend or family business lawyer may offer to represent both you and your husband in a "friendly" divorce. (Most often, this suggestion will come from your husband.) First, God has not yet created a "friendly" divorce. Second, one of you will become the lawyer's enemy before the divorce is over. Third, a husband and a wife with the same lawyer are a husband and a wife with no lawyer. The medical profession's ethics warn against a physician operating on a member of his or her own family. For all the obvious and similar reasons, one attorney should not represent both parties. And most legal canons of ethics prohibit one lawyer representing conflicting interests, and that is what you and your husband have—conflicting interests. Finally, the idiocy of such an arrangement was recognized thousands of years ago in the Bible with the admonition that no man can serve two masters.

2. *Paternalistic or sexist.* It is important that you know your attorney's personal view toward divorce. Has your attorney been divorced and did it color his or her views toward divorce or toward wives or husbands? If a male lawyer, does he regard women as hysterical children? A good divorce lawyer should be gender neutral and regard divorce as an unpleasant but necessary part of the lives of many, who are paying him or her to help them get through as well as they can.

3. *A dazzler.* A good divorce attorney won't try to dazzle you with legal jargon, fancy footwork, and unrealistic promises, leaving you confused as to what has to be done, what it will cost, or what's involved for you. You are interested in competence, not showboating or publicity hype.

4. *An avenger.* The avenger is passionate and dedicated to destroying the opposing party no matter what it costs you both financially and emotionally. She doesn't want to negotiate, she wants to fight. The buzzword is combat, not compromise. This type of gunslinging, macho attorney may appeal to you emotionally because you are in pain and being eaten up with rage inside because that bastard husband is leaving you for another woman or is a drunken bum or has

abused you and the children. Our best advice is that you consider whether you can pay the rent and buy groceries a year from now with vengeance. Not likely. Revenge and scorched-earth tactics in litigation are expensive luxuries that will put you at a tremendous disadvantage in settling the issues in your divorce. Remember, only 2 or 3 percent of all divorce actions filed will go to trial. The rest are settled beforehand through negotiation.

III. HANDLING THE PRELIMINARY INTERVIEW

Take the time and effort and invest the money to interview several prospective attorneys before you decide who can best represent you. Some attorneys will provide an initial consultation without charge and others will charge, but often at a reduced rate. In either case, it is well worth it. You would do the same in selecting a housekeeper or day care for your children or choosing a doctor. Your divorce lawyer will assist you in determining much of what the balance of your life is going to be. Selecting the right one is surely worth a few interviews.

Your interview with each attorney is protected by the attorney-client confidentiality safeguards. A trick that some husbands (and sometimes wives) use is to select the best attorneys in town and interview them as prospective lawyers in the divorce, and in that way preclude them from being hired by the other spouse.

Remember that the preliminary interview is a two-way street and the lawyer is interviewing you at the same time you are interviewing the lawyer. That will allow her to become comfortable with you, as well as you with her. Difficult clients, those who will not listen or whose expectations are simply too high, will not be able to obtain the best legal representation.

A. What You Need to Ask

During the interview, some of the things you need to know and that you should ask if the information is not volunteered include the following:

1. How much of the lawyer's practice is in family law?
2. Who will be handling your case? Will it be the lawyer you are

interviewing or an associate, or will it be the combination of a divorce lawyer and associate or paralegal? This latter is usually the best alternative for you because it provides you with the experienced attorney assisted by the lower-billing associate or paralegal.

3. How much will it cost? While it is extremely difficult for a family law lawyer to estimate fees at the outset of a case, you should know in detail how you will be billed; hourly or at a flat rate (very difficult to do in family law). You must be aware of the hourly rate for your attorney, the associate, and the paralegal who may work on your case. Is there a charge for secretarial time? What is the amount of the retainer, and is the retainer refundable in the event that the time expended does not use the retainer or is the retainer nonrefundable? What is your responsibility for payment of out-of-pocket costs?

Your attorney may be able to give you some average number of hours that will be needed for a preliminary order to show cause and possibly for the drafting of the final agreement and judgment. The reason that it is difficult for a lawyer to estimate fees and costs is because the amount of time that is expended by your attorney is so dependent on how the other side approaches the case. If the other side is going to bombard you and your attorney with burdensome discovery, that will make your attorney's work harder and the case will be more costly. If the other side is hiding assets, finding those assets will be costly. If you need a lot of hand-holding, that, too, will increase your fees.

Remember, you will be charged for your phone calls to your attorney. Prior to calling, make a list of what you need to ask. Don't expect your attorney to resolve every little detail for you. If you have not done so before this, now is the time for you to take hold of your life and think through each decision you will be making in this difficult time in your life and the consequences thereof.

Besides the cost of your attorney and her immediate staff, ask the lawyer what she estimates the total out-of-pocket charges will be and what is included—outside experts, office staff, filing fees, etc.—and what expenses you will be charged for at each stage of the process: preliminary work on temporary orders; investigations, discovery, negotiations; preparing for trial; trial; and after the trial, work on findings and conclusions of law or statements of decision.

4. What is her considered judgment of the outcome?
5. Is she willing to go to court if the case can't be settled?
6. What are alternative arrangements for payment, if any?
7. What does the lawyer expect from you? How can you help with the proceedings?
8. What kind of interim arrangements can be expected for that period between filing for divorce or separation and the final decree, and how will such things be resolved as temporary custody of children, pets, and property; temporary alimony; living arrangements; payment of joint and separate bills and attorney fees?

B. What the Lawyer Is Looking for During Your Interview

As we said, the lawyer will be interviewing you at the same time you are interviewing her. Here are some of the most common traits attorneys look for that make them decide they don't want you as a client:

1. *Signs you will be a difficult client.* Do you appear to be an argumentative, complaining, self-pitying client who will require a lot of hand-holding? Will you be, as we say in the divorce trade, a "high-maintenance client"? This means you will consume vastly more office and staff time than the firm can ever get back in fees, and you will be a losing proposition for them. Such clients are not welcomed by most lawyers and law firms because, regardless of what you have heard to the contrary, law firms are in business to make a profit, and it is difficult to be paid for providing solace, which the client dearly wants at the time but doesn't want to pay for later.

2. *Signs you want vengeance most of all.* If you display signs that you are filled with rage and determined to see that your husband is punished for what he is doing, was doing, and will be doing, you will be unable to hire the best attorneys. The attorney knows that vengeance does not buy lifetime spousal support or a fair settlement, and when all is said and done, a client who presents herself in this manner will bring grief to the lawyer who is bent on protecting the client and not on punishing her husband.

3. *Signs you're a perennial divorce-lawyer shopper.* We urge you to shop around for a good attorney, interview several, and pick one that fits you and your divorce. The extreme of this is the woman who has been shopping around for months or years and has made it into a religion or a hobby. She is actually never going to hire an attorney or secure a divorce and is simply going from attorney to attorney to pour out her grieving heart over the cretin to whom she is married. This is definitely a no-go client for most knowledgeable attorneys. An extension of this is the client who hires an attorney, stays with that attorney for a while, and then, for reasons probably unconnected with what the attorney is doing for her, fires her and moves on to a second, third, or more attorney. Many attorneys will not represent a client who has already gone through two attorneys.

Generally, attorneys want clients who are businesslike, competent, calm, and prepared with necessary information. They want you to appear conservative and ready to do your part of the work that has to be done to get a successful divorce. So come with all the necessary information and be prepared to do what needs to be done.

C. What You Need to Tell the Attorney During the Interview

1. Why you want a divorce.
2. Personal data of the parties: names, home and work addresses and phones, religion, maiden name, social security numbers, age, mental and physical conditions.
3. Marriage statistics: date, place, prenuptial agreements; post-nuptial agreements.
4. Financial details: what is owned and owed; income and expenses; insurance, pensions, long-term obligations, real estate and personal, financial information about your standard of living, how much money is spent monthly on vacations, clothing, gifts, food, transportation, etc.
5. Other parties involved: children, relatives, pets.
6. Cause of breakup: personal, emotional, financial, mental, physical, third parties.
7. Outcome sought: your goals in terms of property or amount of support. It is not helpful to tel! your attorney that you just want your fair share. Be specific as to how you see your joint property divided and how custody and visitation will be handled.

8. If there is a chance for reconciliation through counseling and given a little time.

IV. AVOIDING THE COMMON PITFALLS AND MISTAKES

A. Referral by Interested Party to Divorce

Pleasant and charming as it may sound, do not use an attorney referred to you by your husband or his friends or business associates. Do not use his business attorney, and do not allow him to use a business attorney of his who might have represented both of you in a jointly owned business in the past and is thus in a position of conflict, in a divorce proceeding, to you. Get an attorney on your own, through your own research, and who suits your temperament and needs. When other people, such as your husband's business partner, who have an interest in the outcome of the divorce settlement refer you to their favorite attorney, they are not doing you any favors, no matter how friendly they are to you. Remember, this is not the Community Chest or the Red Cross. Nobody involved in a divorce thinks of it as charity work. It is about money, and you must constantly remind yourself of that or you won't be treated fairly.

B. Both Husband and Wife Using the Same Attorney

This is something we discussed already, but we want to reemphasize it. *It is a no-no.* It is stupid. It is bad. It may be fattening—fattening for your husband's bank account.

C. Enticement by Advertising, Not Ability

Remember that you are hiring an attorney, not a clown or stand-up comedian. Ethically, attorneys may advertise, and there is nothing wrong with that, but use the same care in consulting an attorney as you would in buying a car or a house, because if the divorce goes badly you may be out a car or a house. Subject all attorneys you consider to the same standards of ability and comfort, and don't be misled by flashy advertising.

D. The Do-It-Yourself Kit

The cost of legal services has encouraged the increased use of the do-it-yourself divorce kit and, while there are a limited number of instances where this may suffice, in most instances an attorney is indispensable. Do-it-yourself kits might work in an uncontested divorce where the couple has only been married a short time and there are no kids, property, or other assets to divide and no support issues. However, the minute things start to get sticky or complicated, one of you will run for an attorney, who will probably charge you extra for untangling what you've already done. Oddly, nobody would use a do-it-yourself dental kit, but they will use a do-it-yourself divorce kit and end up with an ache that lasts a lot longer than a few days.

E. Picking a Lawyer on the Basis of Price

The best lawyer for you is not necessarily the most expensive; nor is the least expensive lawyer necessarily the biggest bargain. The most expensive professional you can hire—doctor, lawyer, dentist—is the one that doesn't do the job. The cost of repairing a badly handled divorce is much more than the cost of having it handled correctly the first time. Remember, you are dealing with all you both own in the whole world, along with the custody of your children, pets, stamp collection, Hummel figurines, home, cars, and financial security in the future. How much is it worth to have it done right and to see that you are treated fairly?

F. Hiring on the Basis of Physical Attractiveness

Remember your state of mind and heart when you set out to hire a lawyer. You may very well feel you are a scorned, abused, deserted woman. You may be in a vulnerable position when you meet this drop-dead gorgeous lawyer who is going to free you from that bastard you're married to, and for one and the same price, restore your romantic and feminine self-esteem. Wow! What a package deal! The only problem is that physical intimacy with your lawyer will result in disaster, regardless of what you have seen of the character Arnie Becker on the TV show *L.A. Law*. Whether or not you are treated fairly in your divorce depends on your attorney's ability and not his looks. Neither the opposing side nor the judge is going to be swept away by fantasies of a weekend in the Caribbean with your attorney. If you are choosing a male attorney, choose based on ability—not physical attraction—because too often Mr. Stud turns out to be Mr. Dud in the courtroom.

G. Picking the First Lawyer

It is important that you shop around for an attorney who suits you and your situation. This is, as we said at the beginning of this chapter, the most important decision you will make during the divorce. Take some time, do some research, make the effort initially to find the right attorney, one with whom you will be comfortable and in whom you have confidence. If you have the right attorney, you are halfway to your goal of being treated fairly.

V. WHAT YOUR LAWYER WILL AND WILL NOT DO FOR YOU

She will usually

1. do the legal work.
2. help you keep on track emotionally.
3. help you find the assets of the marriage.
4. craft a settlement if that's possible.
5. try in court matters that can't be settled.

She won't usually

1. do all your work for you.
2. be able to obey court orders for you.
3. resolve irrational emotional problems.

VI. TEN IMPORTANT POINTS TO REMEMBER

In spite of your emotional feelings about the divorce, remember:

1. Normally, neither side can expect to be a complete winner. You will probably not get all you want and neither will he.
2. Marriage is about love. Divorce is about money.
3. She who seeks vengeance should dig two graves—one for her victim and one for herself, because revenge will destroy both of them.
4. Custody of the children is no longer a sure thing for mothers.
5. Do not have sex with your divorce lawyer. Don't pay couch fees.
6. Learn and understand the language of law and accounting.
7. Your lawyer is your lawyer. She is not your therapist, your plumber, your best friend, your lover, your doctor, your car mechanic, your social escort. She is a professional as a lawyer and an amateur at all those other things.
8. It is okay to follow your gut feeling about your lawyer. You must be comfortable with your lawyer because the two of you are going on a rocky voyage together where you may experience seasickness, possibly even fall overboard or hit a reef together. You have to feel good about each other, trust in each other and depend on each other. That means you want a lawyer you are contented with; not your mother, father, or the guy who okays your check at the supermarket.
9. It is important you convey to your lawyer that you want to be told the truth about your case at all times and not just the warm and fuzzy news. If you don't know the truth, you will be unprepared to hear a judge in court agree with some of your husband's positions, and you will be unable to participate meaningfully in the settlement negotiations. You have to know your strengths and weaknesses as well as those of the other side.
10. In the final analysis, you are the person who must make the decisions for you.

CHAPTER FIVE

What to Expect from Your Lawyer

IN THIS CHAPTER YOU WILL LEARN:

> I. What you can expect from your lawyer
> II. How to craft a strategy for a fair divorce
> III. How much money it will cost you
> IV. Danger signs of when to get a new lawyer

I. WHAT YOU CAN EXPECT FROM YOUR LAWYER

A. Respect and Honesty

Here we will discuss your relationship with your attorney, to enable you to understand her role and your own obligations.

First, your attorney is your attorney. As we pointed out in Chapter Four, which deals with the selection of your attorney, she can be expected only to be your attorney and not your psychotherapist or doctor. You are entitled to expect that your attorney will represent you exclusively in your divorce, have no conflicts of interest, and be your advocate both in the negotiations and in the courtroom.

Second, you are entitled to be treated fairly and with respect by your attorney. She should not try to intimidate you, confuse you, or manipulate you. She should treat you as an adult with a problem that she as a specialist will assist you in resolving. She should not embarrass you or ridicule your lack of technical legal knowledge or legal jargon or because you are in a relationship that has not worked out.

Third, your attorney must be honest with you, telling you the truth about the facts in connection with your divorce. There will be some unpleasant aspects of your divorce, and she should be candid about them with you and advise you about the positive aspects of your situation. She will counsel you on what is important to the judge; generally judges are not interested in the other women with whom your husband is sleeping. Judges are interested in dividing property and in assuring that children are properly supported and cared for. You need to be told that in some states, if you are the higher earning spouse, you may be ordered to pay spousal support to your husband. You need to know that you may have to sell the house you have lovingly decorated and redecorated over many years of marriage. In short, you must have an attorney who will tell you the facts that you can reasonably anticipate in starting your new life. You also have the right, for example, to be fully informed of all the costs involved in every step of the proceedings and, in fact, to have these detailed in writing for you. You must know, to the extent possible, what your financial obligations are and what they can be expected to be in the future.

Fourth, your lawyer must acknowledge that the final word on every important decision about your divorce is yours and only yours. Your attorney's job is to advise you about the alternative outcomes of various decisions and help you weigh your choices with the knowledge that, in the end, you must make the decisions because it is your divorce and your life.

Fifth, you have the right to be treated with respect, candor, and courtesy by your attorney's colleagues and staff.

B. Guidance

While the ultimate decisions are yours to make, a good attorney will provide you with clear and firm guidance. She has helped hundreds of others make these decisions; for you it is the first time, and her counsel is essential to your decision-making process.

At the very outset, for example, when you first meet with the attorney, she should tell you what information you need to bring to the meeting so as to make it productive. This should include financial records, income tax returns, records of real estate purchases and sales, bank statements, stock account records, and any financial documents you can put your hands on. She will also suggest you work out a budget showing what you need to support yourself during the divorce process and after the divorce, and to give her information regarding sources of available income.

II. HOW TO CRAFT A STRATEGY FOR A FAIR DIVORCE

Once your attorney fully understands your marital situation and your wishes, she can counsel you on what the best strategy is for achieving the end result that you want.

Your attorney should guide you on your immediate conduct at the beginning of the process and as it continues. She should give you a list of do's and don'ts to direct your conduct. You may have questions about vacating your residence on which your attorney will have thoughts and recommendations. It may not be wise for you to tell anyone about your plans to divorce until your plans are formulated and in progress. It may be that there are a number of things you need to do to protect yourself financially, and in other ways, before everybody knows you are divorcing. A divorce can affect your credit. Therefore, you may want to quietly open new charge accounts and obtain credit cards in your name only while you still have the financial backing of the marital situation. On the other hand, you may want to leave all assets as is in order to create a trusting climate for negotiations between your spouse and yourself and the attorneys. You may want to rent a post office box or mail drop so you can receive mail privately for you only.

In addition to the financial aspects, your attorney can help you in dealing with the emotional consequences. There may be people you need to prepare emotionally for the divorce, such as your own family, your children, and friends. It is best to move carefully to preserve your advantages and to help ease the pain of the breakup. Your attorney can guide you in this, although the ultimate decisions of what to do, and when, are yours. It is generally in the children's best interest that both parents together inform them of the impending divorce early in the process. Whatever you do, try to inform them yourself before they find out from others.

III. HOW MUCH MONEY WILL IT COST YOU?

Naturally, the cost of the divorce is very important to you, and each attorney you interview should spell out the fees and expenses in as much detail as is possible.

There are usually three different ways that attorneys charge for the work they do (expenses and court costs are additional):

A. Time

Most often an attorney will simply charge you for the amount of time she spends on your case. While this may be likened to a taxi meter that keeps running every time your attorney works on your case, it is the most accurate way she has of informing you what she is doing for you and the time expended.

B. Trouble

Attorneys sometimes charge on the basis of the amount of difficulty and complexity involved. A simple, straightforward divorce case involving an uncomplicated estate and relatively amicable custody arrangements will be less expensive, obviously, than a divorce involving a large, complex estate and unusual custody issues. Take the recent case regarding the issue of custody of several frozen fertilized eggs. The outcome of this bizarre case was that the wife received temporary custody of the frozen fertilized eggs. No. We didn't make that up. Clearly the research into these uncharted legal waters would be more costly than research on child custody matters, something that most family law attorneys deal with every day.

C. Final Result

In some kinds of cases, but rarely in divorce matters, an attorney will base his or her fee on the final outcome of the case. This is called a contingency fee arrangement. Here the attorney is paid a percentage of the recovery, usually ranging from one-third to one-half of the money awarded if she wins the case and nothing if she loses. While, the contingency fee arrangement is generally considered unethical in the context of a divorce, there are some instances in which it might be feasible, such as in an investigation to find or collect funds to pay arrearages in support.

In divorce cases, the usual fee arrangement is either of the first two we mentioned: time spent on the case or the trouble involved in resolving it, with the hourly arrangement by far the most prevalent.

You may be charged for the initial interview. Be sure to check with the attorney or her secretary when you make your appointment so you will not be surprised when you are billed for an initial consultation. It could well be worth the cost, even though you will want to interview two or three lawyers before you make your decision as to whom to hire. Some attorneys are willing to meet with you for the preliminary screening interview at a reduced fee or even free, but some charge is not unusual.

During the initial interview, you should discuss the charges and fees that you will be expected to pay as well as anticipated expenses. Surprisingly, some attorneys are reluctant to talk about money, but it is important that the financial arrangements be aboveboard, in the open, and agreed upon before the legal work begins. Otherwise, serious conflict may be created between yourself and your attorney. Indeed, in most states ethical rules are breached when an attorney attempts to negotiate fees after she has taken on your case. Simply ask the attorney you are interviewing candidly what the divorce will cost and what the alternatives are for paying for it.

Most lawyers will ask for a retainer fee as a type of down payment on the work to be done on your matter. This is a fee paid up front before the attorney begins the divorce process for you. This retainer ought to be refundable, and if it is not you should carefully consider whether you need this attorney. By refundable, we mean that if you change attorneys before your retainer is used, or if there is a quick settlement so the cost is minimal, the attorney will refund whatever part of the fee is not used. Your attorney may ask you for a lien on your share of community property to assure payment of her fee.

Invariably, one of the questions you will want answered is what you can anticipate spending to resolve your case. There are at least two problems in giving estimates of fees in this book:

1. There is a lag time between when we write this and when you read it, so the range of fees that might have applied then might be changed now.
2. There is no "typical" divorce. Each has different complexities inviting any number of possibilities, which means the cost will differ for nearly every divorce, even those where the size of the joint estate is comparable.

Having alerted you to these two problems, it is our current experience that attorney fees now run between $150 and $325 an hour. In metropolitan areas rates could run as high as $400 to $450 or more an hour. Even the simplest matter, with no court appearances and no major depositions, probably will require thirty to fifty hours' time to settle. That can give you some sense of what is involved in your case.

On occasion you may find an attorney who will undertake your case for a flat fee, ranging between $2,500 and $25,000. In order to make that type of offer the attorney must be reasonably assured that the divorce will be easily and simply resolved and no court battles are anticipated. This assumes a fairly simple case that can be settled through negotiation, because the minute you get into a courtroom the costs begin to skyrocket.

Another factor in the cost of the divorce is the type of attorney both you and your husband hire. In the real world of divorce, most issues are resolved through negotiation—not showy, dramatic Perry Mason–style trials. So you want to get a specialist in divorce, and if you have to choose between a good negotiator or a hotshot trial lawyer, the good negotiator is the better choice.

Believe it or not, it is also in your best interests that your husband get a competent attorney—one who specializes and understands the process of divorce. If he hires someone inexperienced in divorce law and procedure who just happens to be his business lawyer or golfing buddy, it will slow things down, tend to complicate the issues and eat away at your joint assets.

ONE BIG SECRET ABOUT DIVORCE COSTS

Nobody will probably ever tell you this, but it is a key point you need to understand about your divorce. Generally, the cost of the divorce is going to come out of the total estate that you and your husband have. You and your husband will have what's left to divide. So, the more complicated the case and the more combative the two of you are, the less you will have to divide.

When you have decided upon and hired an attorney, it is wise that you have the details of your relationship—particularly the fees and costs involved—spelled out in writing to avoid misunderstandings. In some states, such as California, your attorney is required to put in writing a fee agreement for any case in which fees will exceed $1,000. In California your attorney must also tell you if she has malpractice insurance coverage. Since the fee in nearly all cases will exceed $1,000, you should have no difficulty getting a written fee agreement. We cannot emphasize the importance of clear understandings and communication between you and your attorney throughout the divorce process, and the way to assure that is to begin the relationship that way.

Your attorney is your champion—your gladiator—in the arena of the divorce conflict. Both of you must trust each other if you are going to be properly represented and survive the divorce. There will be times when you do not understand why your attorney does what she does. Your relationship with your attorney should be such that you can ask her and get clear answers. Often, when there is a barracuda representing your husband, you may want your attorney to behave that same way. A smart lawyer will not lower herself to the level of the scorched-earth practitioner, but she needs to tell you what her game plan is so it can be your joint game plan. Animosity or irritation between the two of you will weaken your position and hurt you. So don't let misunderstandings develop. Keep everything open and clear between the two of you. If you don't like something your attorney is doing or not doing, tell her about it right away. Don't delay. There may be a reason for it that is not immediately evident or she may be confused about your goals. A lawyer who is offended or who expresses surprise that you might question her actions is probably someone you should consider dumping. Lawyers should welcome your inquiries, and a good lawyer will understand if you want to get a second opinion.

First Key Point: If you decide to change lawyers, it is best to have the new lawyer lined up before you fire the old lawyer.

Second Key Point: Most good lawyers don't like to take over another attorney's problems. This makes the initial selection of your attorney extremely important.

IV. DANGER SIGNS INDICATING WHEN TO GET A NEW LAWYER

It can happen that during the divorce proceedings it becomes obvious that you chose not only the wrong husband but the wrong divorce attorney. Just as we don't encourage you to enter into a divorce lightly and without substantive causes, we do not encourage you to change attorneys without careful consideration, because it adds to the expense and the emotional upheaval of the process and makes the entire process a little tougher for you.

Still, there are times when logically you have no choice but to get another attorney. When that moment comes, do it. Do it quickly and decisively and move on with what you need to do. You and your new attorney, of course, are entitled to the documents relating to your case, and your former attorney, of course, is entitled to be paid for the work she has done to date.

Usually, this change of attorneys can be done with little damage to your case, although you must expect that there will be extra fees to bring your new lawyer up to speed on your case. It is unlikely that the judge will be aware of one attorney change in the proceeding, although you can be sure that, if you make attorney swapping a habit, your husband, in an effort to paint you as an unreliable and difficult person, will call that to the judge's attention.

If you get into the game of attorney musical chairs and start changing attorneys with the frequency that you change clothes, a different picture is conveyed to the judge and everybody connected with the case.

Working your way through several attorneys sends out the message that you are flighty, irrational, or unreasonably emotional, or that you take extreme positions. This will work against you in the divorce. Generally it does not work against you in the strictly legal sense, but everybody involved—the other side's attorney, the mediators, the judge—are human and will react as human beings to the signal you are sending. They will get a negative impression of you, and this may hurt your case.

A. She's Not Doing the Job

If your attorney isn't doing her job, then, obviously you need to put a new lawyer on your case. Some clues that she is not on top of your case include repeatedly missing filing deadlines with the court or the opposing attorney; missing settlement meetings or court hearings; or appearing to be unfamiliar with the details of your case and unprepared to properly represent you. Another sign is if you find you can never reach the attorney whom you originally interviewed and are always shunted off to assistants, junior attorneys, or paralegals.

B. She's Insensitive to Your Needs

If your attorney denigrates you and your needs in the divorce, this is a danger sign. If you are not treated with respect as an adult with a problem that you and your attorney will mutually resolve, you probably should be looking for another attorney. This often occurs when a woman hires a hotshot lawyer who has very little regard for the ego or the ability of his client.

C. She Doesn't Communicate

The business of communicating by mail and returning telephone calls in particular is a sensitive area in client-lawyer relations. Admittedly, this is the only divorce you have going at the moment and it is the total focus of your attention, but your attorney will have a dozen or more divorce matters at one time, and she will have to ration her time among all her clients. Therefore, you should be reasonably patient about the return of your telephone calls. On the other hand, you *are* entitled to receive return phone calls from your attorney within a reasonable time. So, if there are inordinate delays in communication by mail or telephone—particularly of important calls and material—your attorney may not be able to handle your needs adequately and you should shop for another representative. You'll know that the delays are unreasonable when your husband shows you material his attorney has received from your lawyer before you receive the same package. Well, it could be the mail—but don't let it happen more than once.

D. You Are in a Divorce Mill

There are some firms specializing in divorce that are organized to make the most money possible out of the divorce *for themselves!* These are known as divorce mills, and they use high-profile, personable attorneys to sign you and then put your divorce into a routine that is handled by low-level paralegals and clerks and may use these mills' expensive expert witnesses whether they are needed or not. Their lawyers often show up for settlement meetings or court hearings ill prepared. This is a production-line type of operation and it is to be avoided.

E. Your Lawyer Encourages Personal Intimacy

We have mentioned the dangers of romantic and sexual intimacy with your attorney before and we'll bring it up again. During the time your divorce is in process, romantic and sexual intimacy with your attorney is a sure invitation to trouble at a time when you don't need any more trouble.

So what's wrong with a little roll in the hay or the payment, as they say in legal circles, of some couch fees? Such behavior can sour the professional relationship between you and your attorney; it is also unethical on the attorney's part and creates a conflict between you. Beyond that, it can really mess up your chance at a fair and expeditious resolution of your divorce. In one case we know, for example, the husband found out about the sexual relationship between his wife and her attorney and sued her attorney for alienation of affections. The wife's attorney had to get an attorney to defend himself, and the wife became involved in two legal conflicts instead of one, all of which adversely impacted her ability to achieve a reasonable settlement in the divorce proceeding. That's a pretty high price to pay for a little fun.

Moreover, in some states a sexual relationship between lawyer and client is specifically prohibited by statute. If your lawyer oversteps, ask him whether his state is one where such conduct might result in his disbarment.

CHAPTER SIX

What Your Lawyer Expects from You

IN THIS CHAPTER YOU WILL LEARN:

I. What your lawyer expects from you
II. The information you need to give your lawyer
III. What you need to do before your divorce is filed

I. WHAT YOUR LAWYER EXPECTS FROM YOU

A. Trust and Honesty

Your lawyer is going to be your colleague during one of the most stressful times of your life, and if that relationship is going to work, you must trust her and be completely honest with her. If for any reason you don't feel you can trust your attorney and be honest with her, you have the wrong attorney. If you feel you cannot be honest with *any* attorney, your first stop might be a psychiatrist.

B. Respect

Just as you are entitled to respect from your attorney, she is entitled to respect from you. Your attorney, if she is being honest with you, will tell you things you may not want to hear and may advise you to do things or *not* to do things that are contrary to your feelings at the moment. It is helpful to remember that this is probably just your one divorce and it may be the hundredth or thousandth divorce for your attorney, who has learned some things about divorce and divorcing people along the way.

So, whether or not you take your attorney's advice or like what your attorney says to you, respect her as a professional who is trying to help you. Your attorney is not unlike your doctor, who may tell you that you have a serious illness requiring surgery or that you must adhere to a specific diet and regime in order to be healthy. You don't have to like what your doctor or divorce attorney is telling you, but you should respect their professional judgment.

C. Realism

Your attorney will expect you to be realistic in your expectations and goals for the divorce. Of course, you are emotionally caught up in the pain of the divorce. Even if you know that divorce is the right path for you, it is an emotionally trying time. You may have been hurt or humiliated or insulted by your husband. You probably have strong feelings about what is fair and what is just, but when you sit down with your attorney to work out the strategy of your divorce, it is time for a reality check. The law is not going to horsewhip your husband or lock him in irons in the village square, punishments that might cross your mind fairly often in the process. The law will not cause him financial ruin nor, in most cases, bar him from ever seeing his children again. The goal of the courts is to see that there is a equitable division of the property and that the children are adequately supported both financially and emotionally.

In fact, if you are the principal wage earner of the family, you may find yourself paying alimony to your estranged husband. You may find that the custody arrangements are not limited to his seeing the children once every two years for lunch. You may be horrified to learn that you may not be awarded custody of the children. Because of the children, you will be forced to maintain a continuing relationship with your ex-husband whether you like it or not. It will be a significantly different relationship, but it will be a continuing one. It could be a better one than that maintained in the last few years of your marriage. When one party obtains custody, generally, the other party will have visitation rights. This will mean regular contact between you and your ex-husband. That is the reality of the situation, and you must be prepared for it and not demand that your attorney change the law for you.

The fact that there will be a continuing relationship and contact with your ex-husband through the interaction of each of you and your children is another reason for being realistic enough to avoid an acrimonious and vengeful divorce. If the two of you can work out a realistic and reasonable divorce settlement, it will make future contacts easier for both of you and, most important, for your children.

It is also important that you be realistic about the divorce process. As we say repeatedly—because it is so, but many spouses find it difficult to accept—the objective of divorce is to undo a marriage and not to gain personal vengeance for either party.

D. Truth About Your Goals

Of all the people involved in your divorce, your attorney must clearly understand what your goals are. By that we mean what your *real* goals are, and not what your family or friends assume or hope they are. Often people assume that the only goal in a divorce is to be legally rid of a bad marriage. While that is the result, it is not always the real or only goal. For example, your real goal may be to forcefully demonstrate to your husband what a price he will pay for losing you. Your real goal may be to play a high-stakes game of chicken to force your husband to end an affair, to pay attention to you, or any number of other objectives that have little to do with the legal termination of the marriage. And, in fact, some women, usually mistakenly, believe that filing for dissolution of the marriage will have just the opposite effect, namely, the strengthening of the marital bonds.

You may want the marriage dissolved and you may indeed have firm and realistic goals about the terms of the dissolution agreement. These usually have to do with money or child custody or other objectives that are important to you. For example, assume you plan to remarry shortly after your divorce is final. That objective must be made known to your attorney (we hope, not to your husband) early on in the relationship so that she can negotiate the settlement for you with that goal in mind.

Nor will all your goals be of equal importance to you; you must make it clear to your attorney what are the goals you *must* achieve in the dissolution of your marriage and, secondarily, the goals you would *like* to achieve. You must explain to your attorney which issues are deal breakers for you; she will then be in the position of advising you what you must sacrifice to obtain those victories. Nothing is gained without giving up something else. Things you would like to have or don't care about become bargaining chips. For example, you may decide that you *must* have $1,500 a month alimony, custody of the children, and the house. You might *like* to have the two dogs, the sofa, and the grandfather's clock, and you *don't care* one way or the other about the time-share vacation condo, the aquarium, and which car you receive.

This is the information your attorney must have when she is negotiating with the attorney for the other side. That other attorney probably has a list of "must haves," "would likes," and "don't cares," too.

II. THE INFORMATION YOU NEED TO GIVE YOUR LAWYER

The information your attorney needs will fall into five categories. Some clients, both men and women, abhor the thought of making lists of assets and obligations, of giving thought to the detail of personal expenses during the marriage and to the future expense level. These clients would rather have the lawyer subpoena the missing information. And, indeed, subpoenas may be served also. However, your failure to do what you can do yourself means that your attorney has to fly blind until information is obtained by subpoena and perhaps expend time and expense you might avoid by gathering the basic information yourself at the beginning. So, take the time; make the effort; get the information so your attorney can do the job representing you that you expect her to do.

Here is a checklist that will help guide you in understanding the kinds of information your attorney needs from you.

A. Personal

Personal information that identifies who the husband and wife are, with a profile about each one. The same is true of the children. This includes dates of marriage and separation, dates of birth and social security numbers. In addition, you need to prepare a brief history of the courtship and marriage.

B. Financial

What is the financial picture of this divorcing couple? In simple terms you should list what is owned and what is owed. It is also important to show what property might be claimed to be separate property as a result of inheritance, gifts, or because it was owned by either husband or wife before the marriage and was kept separate thereafter. Assets that you brought to the marriage or received after the marriage as an inheritance or gift are usually not part of the joint property of the marriage if you have kept it separate in your own name alone, did not commingle it with community funds, or devoted your personal efforts to it without compensation during the marriage. There may be special collections of silver, gems, stamps, coins, china, and/or collectibles that need to be identified, itemized, and evaluated.

If you entered into a premarital agreement, the terms of that agreement and the circumstances under which it was executed become critical information. Bring a copy of the premarital agreement to your first interview with your attorney. Applications for loans or credit can be particularly helpful in financial settlements because your husband will have seen to it that the rosiest picture of his financial condition is painted for the creditor, whereas the tendency in divorce negotiations is to paint the grimmest financial picture. Since loan and credit applications, along with income tax returns, are supposed to be accurate under threat of criminal penalties, they may contain information that can strengthen your bargaining position.

FINANCIAL RECORDS CHECKLIST

- Names and social security numbers of you and your husband
- Place of employment with address, phone, title and details of salary, pension plans, profit-sharing plans, Keogh plans, and other details
- Life insurance of both you and your husband
- Separate property in your separate names
- Real estate (income, business, or investment property)
- Stocks, bonds, and other securities
- Bank and savings accounts
- Debts, liens, and mortgages against these assets
- Joint property
  Real estate (home, income property, etc.)
  Stocks, bonds, and other securities
  Bank and savings accounts
  Debts, liens, and mortgages against these assets
- Details of jointly owned family business
  Other owners, financial statements, loan applications, and income tax returns
- Bank statements
- Income tax returns
- Vehicle registration
- Furniture
- Patents, royalties, and copyrights
- Collections, artworks, and antiques
- Proceeds of legal cases, such as personal injury cases
- Unusual monies, such as lottery winnings
- Trust funds, annuities, and inheritances
- Career assets (allowed in some states). These include seniority, experience, education, licenses or degrees, benefit packages, stock options, deferred compensation, vacation, sick leave, bonuses, etc.

C. Medical

Your lawyer and the court, for support purposes, will want to have records on the medical—physical and mental—condition of each party and the children. Does any member of the family have any disabilities requiring continuing medical attention? Is anybody or has anybody been in therapy for any reason? This information is important in determining alimony, child support, custody, and visitation. You should outline the medical history of you and your husband and all your children or other dependents.

For example, is there a record of mental illness or any hereditary or chronic emotional or physical disorder affecting anybody in the family? Has there been drug or alcohol abuse? Has there been treatment or confinement for any emotional illness, either voluntarily or not? Have there been suicide attempts? You must be prepared to disclose physical, emotional, or sexual abuse of any members of the family. Are there medical, police, or other records available to your attorney that concern any of these problems? These are important issues for your attorney to be aware of in negotiating a settlement or in preparing for trial on issues of support and custody. Your attorney must know about all the facts of your life. The fact that you cannot document these problems does not make them any less real (unless they are not). Be prepared to provide full and complete disclosure of all facts relating to your marriage to your attorney so she can properly represent you. Do not let your attorney be caught unaware of problems when they are raised by counsel for your husband.

D. Special

The first three categories of the information to be supplied to your attorney are fairly straightforward, and probably most of us would have thought about them anyhow. However, there are additional special sources of information you should also collect and preserve because they can have an effect on the financial and custody issues in the divorce. This is information you might not think about that may document infidelity and the use of community assets to further another relationship that undermines the community and fitness to have custody. Your spouse may have kept a diary or notes in a bible that show his recriminations with himself for having severely, too severely, disciplined the children. Even if your case does not go to trial, such information can be helpful in settlement negotiations because the opposing attorney will recognize the effect on the court if the information you have gathered comes out at trial and may decide that it is in his client's best interests to avoid trial, even if the settlement is more costly.

For example, even in those states where the grounds for divorce are fairly simple, such as "irreconcilable differences," and you don't have to prove misconduct by the other party to get a divorce, such misconduct, and particularly misuse of community funds and assets, can sway the balance in the settlement. If a spouse has beaten his wife, had blatant affairs, spent community funds to support those affairs, or mistreated the children, this behavior will affect the terms of the final divorce settlement. Not many spouses obtain their wives' permission to use community funds to buy their girlfriend a fur coat or lease an apartment for her; you must be prepared to fight for reimbursement for community funds spent on others. And mistreatment of you or the children can have a significant effect on custody and on visitation, including whether visitation will be monitored.

Some of the special information you will want to collect and preserve for your attorney includes:

1. *Personal mail.* Your personal mail, and to the extent that you have access to it, your husband's mail, may be helpful to your attorney. For example, you may have letters available that demonstrate your husband's intentions regarding division of the family property or his suitability for custody. There are other forms of communication or indications of mind-set and attitude such as photographs, videotapes, or audiotapes that you should collect. Watch for financial information that comes in the mail. Make your own copies, which you should give immediately to your attorney.

2. *Receipts.* Credit card slips and other receipts showing who spent what, where, and when can be helpful as evidence of misuse of community funds to maintain an extramarital relationship and as evidence of a lifestyle unsuitable for caring for children. Such documents also will establish the family lifestyle, which will show the level of spending for joint expenses. This can be extremely useful information to your attorney as a tool in negotiations.

3. *Canceled checks and bank statements.* Canceled checks are also a good barometer of community lifestyle and the spending habits of both parties. An inordinate number of cash withdrawals or cash checks deserves investigation. Secure the bank statements to establish cash flow and as a means of assuring that you have all the canceled checks.

4. *Telephone, audio, or video recordings.* Telephone conversations, statements made and recorded on audio- or videotape or telephone answering machines can be very valuable if in these conversations the other party agrees to terms of settlement or confesses guilt in a jurisdiction where that is necessary for a divorce. Sometimes spouses will agree in telephone calls to a schedule for visitation or to allow the children to be taken out of the county or state in which they are living, which agreement they later disavow. A recording can be invaluable in these situations.

In most states it is illegal to tape-record a telephone conversation either without the express permission of the other party or without the recording party's ability to prove that she informed the other party of the tape recording and they continued to talk. Thus, it is important that you state on the record that you are recording before beginning the taping.

You may wish to allow your answering machine to screen your calls. You will be surprised at the wealth of information your spouse will leave on your answering machine. Do not make the same mistake yourself. Be wary of voice-activated tape recorders anywhere near your telephone. Your husband can simply leave one of these in the room where you use the telephone. It is turned on and off simply by the sound of your voice. He can retrieve it later and hear what you said on the telephone to your friends, family, *and* your lawyer.

5. *Records of medications.* Drug prescriptions or records of other medications or treatment could suggest that the other spouse is not in any condition to have custody of children. Be aware of what drugs your spouse is using and understand that he will be looking for the same information to use against you.

6. *Calendars and daily diaries.* These can reveal personal lifestyle patterns and possible unsuitability to have custody of the children. Such diaries may show that one spouse was the primary care provider for the children most of the time, which information can affect custody decisions.

7. *Telephone records.* Records of telephone calls can also be important to your attorney to establish contacts, lifestyles, and interests that can be used to trace family assets, and the use thereof, or to establish an unstable child-care situation.

E. Hot Information

This is the hot information that either your husband or you or both of you don't want anybody to know about; information that can explode the divorce settlement sky high if it gets out. This is information that is severely damaging to either side in its claim for money or custody.

For example, records of wrongdoing or suspected wrongdoing such as arrest records, prison records, criminal or civil trials, commitments to mental institutions, or tax evasion may be quite damaging to one or both of you. These could all have a decisive impact on financial and custody questions.

Diaries in which either you or your husband may have kept detailed accounts of very private activities or thoughts could, if discovered, be damaging to either side. In addition, many couples take sexually intimate or incriminating photographs of each other singly or together. Threats to disclose these photographs could have a deleterious effect on the outcome of the divorce from the perspective of the compromised spouse.

In the tough contest of divorce it is to your advantage to secure this hot material from your husband in your possession and control. Likewise, any such material that compromises you, such as diaries, tapes, or photos, should be—all copies—secured by you and either destroyed or safely hidden. In most cases, there will be minimal relevance to these materials, but they will be used to embarrass the other party and force settlement.

In either case, it is important that your attorney know about the existence of such material, whether or not you allow her to read, see, or hear it. If it exists, tell your attorney, otherwise she may be blindsided in negotiations and be unprepared to protect you.

III. WHAT YOU NEED TO DO BEFORE YOUR DIVORCE IS FILED

A. Keep Your Actions Secret

Follow your lawyer's advice; generally it is best to keep the meetings with your attorney confidential between you and your attorney until

---

KEY POINT: SECURE INFORMATION IN A SAFE PLACE

All these documents and information are important to your case, and you should not only gather them but put them in a safe place, beyond the reach of your husband, immediately. Get a safe-deposit box or some other safe depository. Don't leave important documents with relatives or friends who may turn against you. If you have the time, it is smart to make copies of everything and put the copies in a secure place. Excessive precautions? No. The outcome of your divorce depends on your having control of this information.

---

such time as you are ready to make a move. Obviously, you don't want your husband to know until the appropriate time, and that means neither your children nor your close family or friends should know until you are ready to let him know. If you have to account for your time (which in itself bodes ill for you), you can feign a routine medical check or shopping. There are good reasons for this:

1. *You may change your mind.* One obvious reason is that you may change your mind and decide that you don't want a divorce. If you decide against a divorce and your husband finds out that you have been consulting a divorce attorney, it could have unpleasant or embarrassing repercussions and impede your effort to make the marriage work. Of course, you will want to pay your attorney in cash or in some way that doesn't leave a paper trail back to you that your husband might discover. Maintaining the confidentiality of your early meetings with your divorce lawyer is important for many psychological and practical reasons.

2. *You want to prevent your husband's preemptive counterstrikes.* Another major reason for keeping your early moves confidential is that, if you don't, your husband may immediately make a preemptive strike that harms your interests. For example, he might cancel charge accounts, strip all the money out of bank accounts, move to hide assets, seize and conceal important family assets, and even attempt to leave with the children. Or he might secrete financial records to make it harder for you to collect information to insure you are treated fairly in the divorce.

3. *You want to prevent physical or sexual abuse.* For some men, the threat of a divorce and radical alteration of his lifestyle, attack on his assets, and the public embarrassment of the divorce action may trigger a violent and abusive physical or sexual reaction. This is another reason to keep things confidential until you are ready and in a position to protect yourself.

4. *You need to establish a strong position.* A divorce is the ultimate power struggle between you and your husband. To assure your success, you must put yourself in a strong bargaining position whether you are a working wife or a full-time mother and homemaker. To establish a strong bargaining position, you need some time to gather information and documentation that your attorney can use in negotiations with your husband's attorney. We have already talked about some of the information, documentation, and actions you need to take and will detail even more as we go through the divorce process. Your lawyer will undoubtedly counsel you on a number of strategic moves you need to make before filing and going public with the divorce. But you need some time to work with your attorney in confidence before the breakup of your marriage becomes public knowledge and your family and friends start to take sides.

5. *You want to prevent premature emotional upset of children and others.* By letting the word out about the divorce too soon, you may upset your children, your family, your friends and others before you've had time to lay the groundwork emotionally with them. This is important for the mental stability of the children and for others you may need to rally to your side of the conflict.

B. When to Go Public

There are, of course, circumstances that may force you to go public with the divorce because you and your attorney cannot control every aspect of the dissolution procedure. These include:

1. *Your spouse begins making countermoves.* If your husband suspects or learns about your intentions (usually this is easy to do), he may begin to make countermoves, such as trying to raid your joint bank account, canceling joint charge accounts and credit cards, and, in general, attempt to dry up the money that is available to you. Also, he will try to grab all the records he can and take them out of your reach. He will try to do these things without arousing your suspi-

cions. If you discover that your husband is making such counter-moves, you should consult your attorney and seriously consider going public with the divorce immediately and moving quickly to obtain preliminary court orders to protect your assets.

2. *Your husband becomes violent or abusive.* If your husband begins to be violent or abusive toward you and the children, you should take action immediately. Consult your attorney and obtain move-out and stay-away orders. You can also do this before you have found a lawyer. In some states, at the moment any violence occurs call 911 immediately and describe the abuse. Generally the police will be able to provide you with immediate emergency protective orders.

C. What Not to Do Before Filing for Divorce

There are several things your attorney has the right to expect that you will not do because this type of conduct will undermine her ability to represent you properly, among them:

1. *Do not move out of the house.* Moving out of the family residence can seriously affect your bargaining position and, perhaps, custody of the children. In most cases your attorney will advise you to stay in the family home. Traditionally, it is the husband who moves out, and unless there is some insurmountable problem, let him do that and you stay in the house. You may find, however, that your husband has been advised by his lawyer not to move out of the house, making the living situation quite difficult for both of you. You and your attorney will have to plan your strategy, but in no event should you move out without planning that strategy.

2. *Do not communicate with your spouse's lawyer.* Under no circumstances should you ever communicate directly with your spouse's attorney or his colleagues or staff, or with the court or others officially connected with the case. This weakens your attorney's negotiating position by demonstrating that the other side can go around her and, therefore, doesn't have to pay attention to what she says. In most jurisdictions, communication between a client and the opposing attorney when that client is represented by counsel is a breach of professional ethics.

3. *Do not fight with your husband.* It is always unwise to lose your temper or quarrel with your husband. It is your attorney's job to

work things out with your husband's lawyer, and it is the job of your husband's attorney to obtain your husband's compliance with preliminary and temporary agreements made by the lawyers. If you get into a shouting, name-calling match with your husband, again you undermine the authority of your advocate, to say nothing of demonstrating that you are emotionally volatile. At worst, your conduct might be such to justify a vindictive spouse's filing a criminal complaint against you for threats, battery, assault, and a variety of other charges that will divert attention from the real issues in the dissolution proceeding.

4. *Do not have sexual intercourse with your husband (or anyone) during the pendency of the divorce.* Certainly after the divorce action is filed, you should not have sex with your husband. In some jurisdictions, the very act of having sex with your husband after you have filed the divorce may, in effect, nullify the divorce action because you are indicating a preference to continue the marital relationship. If you then continue with the divorce proceedings, your husband might use your sexual encounters with him against you.

If you begin having a sexual relationship with someone else during the divorce and your husband produces proof of that to the court in the form of private detective reports, film, audio recordings, and the like, it will do more than embarrass you; in some jurisdictions it could jeopardize your chances to be awarded child custody and might influence the court to decide against you, however subconsciously, on close questions.

It should not be necessary to warn you again against having sex with your divorce attorney.

CHAPTER SEVEN

Your Children and Your Divorce

IN THIS CHAPTER YOU WILL LEARN ABOUT:

I. Types of custody arrangements and understanding custody
II. Preparing for some unpleasant truths about custody
III. Dealing with telling the kids
IV. Obtaining the best support arrangement

I. KINDS OF CUSTODY AND HOW YOU CAN HANDLE IT BEST

There are often other living creatures involved in a divorce besides you and your husband. In fact, every year in the United States there are 624,400 divorces that involve minor children and decisions on the issue of custody. Many cases involve custody issues between birth parents and adoptive parents, other relatives, and gay or lesbian couples.

A. Understanding Custody

There is a wide range of psychological reasons for custody disputes between parents, and we mention these only briefly to put your custodial situation in perspective because the impetus behind custody battles could fill a book. Sometimes the reasons are as simple as a parent loving his or her children and sincerely believing that it is in their best interests to remain with that particular parent to the virtual exclusion of the other. There are other occasions where the reasons are more complex, and perhaps not connected with the well-being of the children at all. Having custody of the children may help to ease one through the difficult emotional transition in life that comes with divorce. Sometimes the child is a surrogate for the lost love and affection that once was in the marriage. And, too often, the child is a pawn being used to obtain revenge or to hurt the other person. A husband may want to deny his soon-to-be ex-wife custody of their children so as to punish her or hold her up to humiliation in the community. A husband or wife may want custody to prove that he or she is the injured party in the divorce and, now, is the martyr trying to preserve what is left of the family. In jurisdictions where there is a large differential in the amount of child support paid, depending on the custodial time enjoyed by the noncustodial parent, the reasons for seeking more custodial time may be financial.

Traditionally, custody of the children has been awarded to the wife because of the stereotype that women are the more nurturing of the two parents. In fact, even today mothers who do not seek or obtain custody of their children are criticized as being uncaring mothers, or in cases where the court makes an order awarding custody to the father, mothers may be characterized as unfit. Too frequently we find that being an unfit mother is a greater transgression than being an unfit father. Yet the reality of our modern American industrial society is that the mother does not always obtain custody of the children, nor, in some cases, should she.

At the heart of the problem are the inconsistencies in the law. There are fifty states, plus several territories and other political entities, each of which has its own statutory scheme for awards of custody and case-made law regarding custody. This makes for enormous differences, and in some cases where parents cross state lines, for general chaos.

The law of child custody in America is in a state of flux, particularly when the court is considering custody between birth parents, as a couple and individually, and nonbirth parents. We saw that in the sad tale of "Baby Jessica" in 1993, when the sobbing little girl was taken away from her adoptive parents in Michigan and given to her birth parents in Iowa, to the shock and outrage of millions of people around the country. That was a high-profile case with significant media attention. There are thousands of other cases that get less attention but cause just as much heartbreak.

For example, in recent months a judge in Macomb County, Michigan, took three-year-old Maranda Ireland-Smith away from her mother, Jennifer Ireland, because the mother put Maranda in a day-care home while she worked. Custody was given to the natural father, Jennifer's ex-boyfriend Steven Smith, in spite of Jennifer having charged him with child abuse. Smith's mother will care for Maranda at her home. This lower court order was stayed pending a ruling by an appellate court, but this mother stands in danger of losing her child because she is living what is supposed to be the American way, improving her education to obtain better work and caring for her child by the only means available to her. In Virginia, the court took two-year-old Tyler away from his lesbian mother, Sharon Bottoms, and her live-in partner, ruling Bottoms was an unfit mother. On appeal, the ruling was reversed and Tyler is back with his mother again. In Illinois, the court took a three-and-a-half-year-old boy away from the adoptive parents who had cared for him since birth and gave the child to the natural father.

Andrea Stone, writing in the July 29, 1994, *USA Today,* summarized the present dilemma over custody in our court systems—or rather, our fifty-plus state court systems. "The cases underscore the nation's growing debate: how to define a family, who is a good parent and what is in a child's best interest. But they also raise troubling questions about the guidelines used to award custody which vary state to state and the power that judges asked to play Solomon may wield."

Lynne Gold-Bikin, the head of the American Bar Association's family law section, observes: "Judges have enormous discretion. You can take the same set of facts and put them in front of five different judges and get five different results."

It is so important for you to understand that point that we want to repeat and emphasize it: *You can take the same set of facts and put them in front of five different judges and get five different results.*

Some of the factors contributing to the widespread confusion over child custody is the growing and heated political debate over the issue of "family values," in which there are great differences of opinion as to what is in the best interest of the child. In addition, there is a huge market for adoptive children, particularly white infants, and the pressure and vast amounts of money to be made sometimes have adoptions hastily made and leisurely repented in front of a judge when the birth parents change their minds. Beyond all this is the recognition and acceptance by the courts of differing lifestyles, which suggest that the biological parents are not always best for the child and that gay couples can be loving, caring parents, too.

The point is that the old rules are out the window, and if you want custody today, you had better do your homework, make a strong case for your version of what is in the best interests of your children, and be prepared to spend the money necessary to fight for custody of the children.

Custody of the children is usually a touchy situation, and it can end up in some strange arrangements. One of the most unusual that we have encountered was the Alice and Charlie situation. Alice married Charlie, who had custody of his two children by his first marriage to Charlotte, who had deserted the family and couldn't be found. Alice and Charlie divorced, and the court ruled that Charlie was not a fit parent and awarded custody to Alice, who then married Joe. The final order had the natural children of Charlie and Charlotte in the custody of Alice and Joe, neither of whom was the parent of the children. However, most custody cases ultimately result in a custodial situation where one of the natural parents is the primary custodial parent and the other parent has time with the children, which may range from every other weekend to one-half of the children's time. The Alice-Charlie-Charlotte-Joe situation is not the norm.

B. Types of Custody: Temporary and Permanent

Upon separation, you and your husband will be forced to deal with the issues of temporary custody. The fact is that during the interim period after separation and prior to the order dissolving your marriage, the court, in considering the issue of temporary custody, will strive to maintain the status quo that the children have enjoyed during the time that their parents are together. Thus, you have one of the most cogent reasons for remaining in the family residence. That is the children's home; if you move out without the children, you run the risk of your husband being awarded temporary custody because he is there and there is no reason why he cannot care for the children. If you move out and take the children with you, you are toying with the status quo of the children and you must be prepared to give an extraordinarily good reason for removing the children, such as physical abuse to them or to you. The goal of temporary custody is to avoid disruption in the lives of the children of the divorcing spouses.

Permanent custody is granted at the time of the dissolution of the marriage. One of you may be awarded permanent physical custody or perhaps both of you will be awarded shared physical care of the children, with the periods of sharing being spelled out as to when the children will be with each parent.

Within these two custodial situations, there is a range of types of custody that can be awarded or agreed to between the two of you, among them:

1. *Legal custody: sole legal custody versus joint legal custody.* Sole legal custody means that one parent alone is given the authority to make all the important decisions about the child's life until the child becomes an adult. The other parent becomes a cipher in these important issues. The fact that one parent has sole legal custody does not generally impact the visitation rights of the other parent, but decisions about where the kids go to school or church, where they live, who provides medical care and other essential services are at the sole discretion of the parent having sole legal custody.

In most situations, joint legal custody is the most common custodial order, so that both parents can share equally the responsibilities of deciding on education, religious affiliation, and nonemergency medical care. In essence, it lets the parents divorce each other without divorcing the parents from the children. Obviously, this can create some stressful situations where the divorced parents cannot tolerate each other and cannot, or more likely will not, cooperate in the raising of their children. Joint legal custody does not deal with the primary residence of the children. It is provided to give the parent who does not have primary physical custody some input in the raising of the children. The agreement between you and your husband should specify what decisions are to be joint decisions.

2. *Physical custody.* In most states the trend is to provide for joint physical custody with specific times of custodial care to one of the parents. The theory is that the best relationship for the children is to be around both parents, even though this type of sharing may not be what the parents had anticipated. In essence, the children still enjoy the company of two parents, even though mother and father are no longer husband and wife.

Obviously, this is not an ideal arrangement for you and your ex-husband if either or both of you has not been able to come to terms with the fact of divorce and getting on with your separate lives. However, most parents are able to recognize the benefit to their children from frequent contact with both parents and deal with that to the benefit of the children. But there are those who don't ever reach that point, and in those cases joint physical custody may not be an option.

There is often confusion about what "joint custody" means in the real world. This may be because the law doesn't specifically define joint custody. Generally, it does not mean that the children spend exactly the same amount of time with each parent. The children never did this even when their parents were still married. It does mean that it will be more difficult for either parent to move away from the area in which both are living at the time that this custodial arrangement came into existence.

3. *Sole physical custody with visitation to the noncustodial parent.* In most jurisdictions, the most common type of physical custodial arrangement is sole physical custody to one parent with the other having visitation rights that are spelled out in the decree. The parent with sole physical custody is presumed to have the day-to-day responsibility for the children; when the other parent has the children with him, it is assumed that he will have primary responsibility for the children.

4. *Split custody.* Split custody is where all the children live with each parent part of the time or where some children live with one parent all the time and other children live with the other parent all of the time. In other words, it implies a splitting up of the siblings, which is usually not desirable for the children, particularly for pre-teen children. Splitting the time by dividing it into great chunks of time, which is also considered a form of split custody, may be considered when the two parents are living in widely separated locations and it makes more sense for the children to spend several months with one parent instead of trying to visit every weekend. Sometimes the children will live for one year with one parent and the next with the other. It has the psychological advantage for many children in that it provides for the continuity of living in one place without frequent shuttling back and forth. For the parents, it also provides each of them with reasonably long breaks away from the responsibility of the children while still knowing they are being well taken care of by the other parent. Obviously, it will have an impact on the continuity of education.

TAKING CHILDREN OUT OF STATE

Usually, a parent may take his or her children out of the state and beyond the jurisdiction of the court only if there is no custody proceeding pending. If a custody action has been filed, written permission of the court or the other parent is required to take children out of the state.

II. PREPARING FOR SOME UNPLEASANT TRUTHS ABOUT CUSTODY

A. Custody Is Sometimes Controlled by Outsiders

Let's start with a touch of the real world by examining the American court system. You will learn some things you may not like, especially if you are putting your fate in that system. In spite of lawmakers', judges', and society's best intentions, most court systems in this country are tremendously overloaded and ill equipped to handle sensitive custody decisions. This forces courts to adopt procedures that may be less than perfect. This is a reality for divorce cases as well as for all noncriminal cases, such as business disputes and personal injury matters.

It would be nice if a wise and kind judge could sit for several hours and listen to you and your spouse rationally discuss the pros and cons of who should get custody, but the truth is that the judge won't have more than a few minutes to decide these most significant issues in your and your children's lives. So, in more and more instances, the courts are appointing psychologists or family counselors to evaluate which custodial arrangement would best serve the interests of the children. Sometimes counselors are charged with the duty of assisting the parents in working out a custody agreement between them. In other courts, where counselors are used, they act as judges. They will talk with the parents and the children, sometimes administer some psychological tests, and then make their recommendation to the judge, who will make an order based on that recommendation. Although judges have the power to overrule the counselor, the fact is that they do not often do that. It's the easy, fast way to resolve custody cases, and in the great majority of cases these trained professionals are well equipped to handle this difficult job. However, you must be aware of who has the last word in these issues. Ask your attorney. Don't go into any interview with a third party without knowing precisely his or her role in your case.

The decision regarding custody is not strictly a legal issue. As you can see, considering that psychologists and marriage and family counselors are involved in the decision making, a great deal depends on the degree of psychological bonding between the parents and the children; the extent to which one parent recognizes the need of the children to have regular and frequent contact with the other parent, and the custodial parent's ability to recognize his or her own self-worth independent of his or her role as parent to the children. The counselor will carefully observe the behavior of the children around each parent and the messages that such behavior carries.

B. No One Automatically Gets Custody

For many years an award of custody to the mother was an automatic conclusion. Society's values reflected a family structure composed of a father who supported the family and a mother who stayed at home, kept house, and raised the children. Society changed, and that change is reflected in changes in the law and in court rulings that now consider the best interests of the child in awarding custody, and often, although not yet on a 50/50 basis, are awarding custody to the father. The "traditional" family structure is no longer the norm; most women work outside the home and a great number of families are headed by single working parents.

The concept today is that primary custody of the children generally should go to the parent who, despite the fact that he or she is working outside the home, is still the more nurturing parent, the one who takes time off to visit the schools, who attends the children's functions, who picks up and delivers, and who keeps regular hours most suitable for time with the children. The same is as true of fathers, more of whom are seeking custody, as of mothers.

The stated objective of the court system is to protect the best interests of the children in custody battles by awarding primary cusody to the parent who is the most able to place the needs of the children, and indeed of the other parent, before his or her own. Obtaining and maintaining custody is a difficult task in these modern times.

You will be asked by your attorney to provide a list of witnesses who can attest to specific incidences of your participation with the children in their activities, that you are the parent who dressed, bathed, and fed the children; took them to school; attended school functions; took them to the doctor; took them on recreation trips; bought and cared for their clothing; spent time with them on homework; and was generally the main caregiver for the children. For example, checks and credit card receipts for children's clothing, medical expenses, and entertainment signed by you can prove you were there caring for them. You may be able to document that your husband was entertaining himself and traveling away from home and not available to care for the children. Your husband's answer to this will be that he was the wage earner and forced to be away from home. He will present a new work schedule that will provide him significant time with the children and less time at work. Be prepared to welcome these changes in his life with open arms. In most instances it won't last long, and it will not preclude your being named primary custodial parent. Your willingness to promote your ex-spouse's time with the children will show you as the more understanding parent, willing to share. And there may come a time when you will welcome a respite from the children.

C. Custody Fights Are Not Best for Children

It is a sad commentary on us as parents that we do not always put the best interests of our children first. A custody battle in itself bodes ill for the children, since it tells the court and all others involved that the parents are incapable of resolving their mutual differences, even when it comes to looking for the best for their children. Too often the professed concern for the children masks a desire to hurt the other parent or to lower or increase child support payments. For example, if your husband knows that you are willing to sacrifice anything to have sole legal custody of the children, he will use this knowledge as a bargaining chip to force you into an unfair financial settlement.

Husbands and wives fight over custody of the children, not out of care and concern for the children, but for motives of revenge or greed. One spouse seeks to hurt the other by undermining the relationship between the children and the other parent and instigating a custody fight in an attempt to take the children away from the other spouse. This type of activity without something more will usually not be successful, but it will cause great emotional turmoil for the other spouse and put that spouse in a weak position for bargaining on other issues. This battle is not about the children. It is about revenge, guilt, abandonment, and rejection. Or you may be motivated to deny your husband custody because of your own devastation as a result of the new woman in his life, and that this woman may be helping to raise the children, who are all you have left of a shattered marriage.

Greed is another distasteful human trait that is commonly found in divorce. Sometimes hunger for the money is part of revenge and sometimes it is part of reality and need, but whatever the reason, greed often enters into custody battles. Your husband may figure he may pay less child support to you if he has primary custody. And he is right. Sometimes there are the subtle pressures exercised by a grandparent who has money, and on behalf of her child, your ex-husband, will provide him with the financial resources to wage the custody battle. That grandparent may even become personally involved to the extent that your kindly mother-in-law is now your worst enemy.

Sometimes children are the recipients of sums of money, perhaps from grandparents or from other sources, and the desire for custody is really the desire to have control of the children's money. This has produced some strange lawsuits, including unusual divorces. We have already seen the case where husband and wife fought over the custody of nine frozen fertilized eggs that the couple had created and stored in happier days. The wife's objective was to enable her to give birth to a child sired by her ex-husband. That the child would be eligible to inherit from the ex-husband's estate was probably incidental because the father could write the child out of his will. A similar case, involving not divorce but greed, generated a court case by the heirs of a South American couple killed in a plane crash, leaving behind an estate in the hundreds of millions of dollars and a set of fertilized eggs in a clinic freezer. Relatives fought for custody of those eggs so they could be destroyed and never used to produce more heirs to compete for the couples' fortune. Extreme examples, sure, but they demonstrate the same motivations that are replayed in courtrooms around America every day.

A DIFFERENT POINT ON THE SAME SUBJECT

A lot of what is said about children in this chapter can also apply to pets. Some people are surprised by how seriously divorcing couples will battle over custody of favorite pets, but it happens all the time.

D. Children Can Be Witnesses in the Divorce

It is legally possible for some children to be witnesses at a divorce trial, and you should be prepared for that possibility. Each court and state will determine the suitability of a child witness in terms of maturity and age in weighing that child's competency to be a witness in a court trial.

However, from the standpoint of the well-being of your children, their testimony at a custody trial is usually to be avoided at nearly all costs. Bringing the children into that adversarial confrontation between the two parents as a witness for one side or the other pits that child against the other parent, causing, in most cases, grave psychological damage to the child. This is true no matter how persuasive the child is that he or she be allowed to testify. It would be difficult to find an expert in the field of child psychology who would recommend putting a child through the trauma of appearing in a courtroom to testify against one of his or her parents. The impact on the child can last long after the divorce is over and ultimately may cause the child, as he or she becomes more mature and begins to understand the motives of the parent for whom he or she testified, to blame that parent for the child's certain estrangement from the other parent. Remember, children need both parents.

Despite the recognized dangers of these tactics, your husband may try to convert one or more of your children to "his side." Be alert to this possibility or the threat that your husband might use this as a lever to force concessions from you.

E. Kids Can Have Some Say About Custody

The children's best interests are the fundamental objective of custody decisions, and, the older the children are, the more likely their opinions will be taken into account by the court. Not every judge will meet with a child, but those who do generally say that they will consider the custodial desires of children between twelve and fourteen. (After age fourteen, if a child does not want to visit or live with a particular parent, it is nearly a lost cause to try to change the child's mind.) Parents are often surprised to learn belatedly that their children are frustrated and angry because no one is willing to listen to them, and in some cases children who are bold enough and have enough confidence in themselves have asked to speak privately to the judge. In many cases, judges will appoint an attorney to represent the children's interests in court. This may occur if the attorney for the mother or father decides to call the child as a witness.

F. The Molestation Tactic May Come into Play

The law and the courts are no more immune from fads and trends than any other part of society, and one of the more disturbing trends in custody battles is for one parent to charge the other with sexual molestation of the children.

Obviously, if there has been sexual molestation of the children by a parent, it is the moral obligation of the other parent to report it immediately. If there has not been sexual molestation, however, making the false charge is truly shameful because it can tarnish the reputation of an innocent person and mark the life of the child forever.

Molestation charges have destroyed the reputation of teachers, parents, and others all over the country in recent years, and even when proven false, the stigma remains. In cases where the charge of molestation is proven, often one is left wondering why the accusing parent did not come forward long before the divorce. In some instances, the circumstances have been headline grabbing, such as the McMartin preschool case, the Menendez brothers murder case, and the Morgan case in Washington, D.C., where the mother went to jail for months rather than reveal the whereabouts of her daughter, whom the mother charged the father with molesting.

Whatever the facts or the motivation of child molestation charges, one should understand that it is a terrible charge to bring without proof, and it is reasonably difficult to prove in many cases. Psychologists who examine such children, for example, tend to hedge their conclusions because they often cannot know for sure what happened. Moreover, if such a charge is made it will open a Pandora's box of consequences that cannot always be foreseen.

G. Neither Parent May Get the Kids

Even more surprising to divorcing parents than the fact that the mother doesn't automatically get the children is the startling fact that it is possible that neither will obtain custody. It is possible that the judge, in reviewing the case, may find that neither parent is competent to care for the children. The judge may appoint an attorney for the children to represent their best interests. In that case the attorney is obligated to recommend to the court that the best interests of the children will be served by placing them with neither of the parents but rather with, for example, a grandparent or aunt or uncle.

There is also the possibility that another relative may petition the court for custody of the children on the grounds that neither parent is competent to care for the children, or that their best interests will not be served by placement with either parent.

III. TELLING THE KIDS

Telling the children about the divorce is tricky business at times. Most parents have less incentive to tell the children about an impending divorce than they have to tell them about the facts of life. Of course, divorce is another fact of life; often parents who are sure they have been successfully concealing their marital problems will be startled to learn that their children knew about the divorce long before their parents found it in themselves to tell them. Most children are not stupid, and they don't live on another planet. They learn at an early age how important it is to psyche out what their parents are thinking and doing and probably know about the divorce or strongly suspected it was coming before anybody tells them officially.

In any case they have to be told "officially," and it is important that you tell them as a couple, as their parents together providing reassurance of your continued love for them. Consulting a therapist may be a good idea to help you approach the problem. Reading a parenting book will be helpful. Here are a few pointers. Think about it in advance. Discuss it with your spouse and decide how, what, and when to tell your children together.

A. Assure the Kids You Love Them

It is universally agreed by experts that children often see the breakup of the two parents as meaning that they are at fault, and one or both of the parents do not love them. Give your children strong assurances of your love for them and particularly reassure them that they—the children—are not the cause of the divorce. There is considerable psychological damage to the children if they feel they are to blame for the divorce. Their guilt may be fostered by one or both of you when you cannot accept responsibility for the divorce, and each of you wants to reproach someone else for your own failures. You and your husband should both pledge that you will always be there for your children, and you should each mean it when you make that promise.

B. Try To Be Unemotional

However difficult it may be to control your own emotions when you are telling the children, it is best not to overdramatize the divorce or make it into a disaster. Essentially, it is a situation in which two people no longer get along and are uncomfortable living with each other. That happens; it will be a catastrophe only if you make it so.

C. Keep It Simple and Honest

Don't overestimate how much your children want to know. Often children prefer to be spared too many of the gruesome details. There is a story about a young child asking his father where he came from; the father sat the child down and gave him a four-hour lecture about human reproduction. At the end, the father asked the boy what prompted the question. The boy replied, "Oh, Ralph next door said he came from Detroit, and I just wondered where *I* came from."

Again, it is not unusual that the children have seen it coming, and often they are glad that finally the "D" word is in the open. It could mean a more peaceful life for children who have been living in a household of constant argument and tension between the parents. In that sense, the kids may actually welcome the separation if not the divorce.

D. Try to Keep Them from Taking Sides

Do not force the children to take sides in the divorce. Often they will be anxious about their role in the proceedings, and you and your spouse must tell them that they have none other than what specifically concerns them. Tell them they will not be involved in the proceedings—if that is true—and that their lives will be disrupted as little as possible: They'll continue to go to the same school, have the same friends, live in the same place, and they will see the "out" spouse often. Discuss the schedule for visitation with them. Remember that you are getting a divorce from their father, but they aren't. Soon he will no longer be your husband, but he will always be their father, just as you will always be their mother. Do not lie to your children. Do not paint a picture of life after divorce that simply cannot be. Children will be more damaged by lies from their parents than by the truth, however difficult it may be for them to accept. If you are the noncustodial parent, never, never tell the kids you will be there and then fail to show up.

E. Listen to Your Kids

It is usually a good idea to let the children have their say about what's going on, however emotional and angry they may be about it. However, our experience is that you should be prepared for the unexpected. You may be startled, even embarrassed when you hear what your own kids have to say about you and your husband, the marriage, and, now, the divorce. They have independent minds and may have drawn conclusions about your marriage that you never dreamed they thought about. This could be a major reality check for you. It is also a wonderful opportunity to empathize with your kids and their feelings, to bond with them and do some healing that might be more necessary than you suspected.

IV. HOW TO BARGAIN FOR THE MOST EQUITABLE SUPPORT

If you are the parent who is awarded primary physical custody of the children, you normally will be entitled to receive financial help from your husband to assist you in supporting the children. In some cases the custodial parent may be ordered to pay child support to the noncustodial parent who has no or limited income so that parent can enjoy the children while they are with him or her and provide a home that can accommodate the children for visits. In this day and age custody may be given to the father if the mother is the principal wage earner who herself has not had the time to be the principal caregiver to the children. It's a changing world, and we must learn to adjust to it.

You and your attorney should be prepared to demonstrate the financial resources of the paying parent to show his ability to pay adequate child support. Don't be deluded into thinking that the paying parent will be required to pay all of the expenses of caring for the children. You will be expected to contribute to their maintenance and care, too.

IMPORTANT POINTS TO CONSIDER IN CHILD SUPPORT NEGOTIATIONS

- Include a provision in the child support order to require that minor children be included in the paying parent's will and life insurance policy.
- Try to get minor children's support tied to increases in the paying parent's salary, income, trust fund, bonuses, stock options, and raises.
- Regardless of who gets the custody of the children, if he or she is financially entitled to child support, it is worthwhile for that parent to do her homework on what the cost of taking care of the child will be.

IMPORTANT POINTS ABOUT CHILD SUPPORT

- It continues only while the child is a minor, which is normally until age eighteen. In some states, child support continues until the child is twenty-one.
- Child support payments are not taxable to the parent who receives them and not deductible for the parent who pays them.
- It is not necessary to be divorced or to have been married to be entitled to child support in most states. Child support is for the benefit of the child and has little to do with parental status.

Carefully list and document all the normal expenses of raising the children, including the basics: food, clothing and shelter, education, medical care, recreation, dental care, insurance, therapy, gifts for birthday parties, video rental, vacations, and camps.

The method of calculating child support will vary from state to state. However, in the early 1980s every state adopted guidelines for child support under pressure from the federal government. These guidelines call for child support of 17 percent of the paying parent's income if there is one child to support; 25 percent if there are two children; 29 percent for three children; and up to 35 percent for a maximum of five children. These percentages are required on the first $80,000 a year the paying parent earns, and additional support is at the discretion of the court.

We conclude this chapter by noting that, just as the circumstances of our lives change with time, so do the details of child custody and child support. Obviously, the laws of each state continue to evolve in response to changing conditions in society and shifting pressures on legislators. Children inevitably grow up, and at some point will be making their own decisions about which parent they want to live with regardless of what the parent's wishes are. Parents' lives change, too, with shifts in employment, new personal relationships, and differences in age and health.

So, too, there is room for changes in custody and child support arrangements. If the paying parent loses his or her job, no amount of court orders will produce the support the child needs. If you have custody of the children and remarry, your new financial situation might, in some jurisdictions, justify a modification in the child support payments required of the other parent. And if you or the other parent wish to move away and take the children, that creates the most heart-wrenching of custodial cases.

What we are telling you is that rarely is the child custody and child support order that you thought was final at the time of the divorce "final." Be prepared—if you and your ex have children, you will be sleeping together until they are at least eighteen years of age and sometimes longer.

CHAPTER EIGHT

Money and the Divorce Treasure Hunt

IN THIS CHAPTER YOU WILL LEARN:

> I. Facts, tricks, and unsavory truths about the money
> II. What financial records are important to you
> III. Protecting your financial interests
> IV. Finding the money he's hiding from you

As we said earlier, if marriage is about love and devotion, divorce is about revenge and money. We try to avoid dealing with revenge in the courts of law and in this book, but we do spend some time talking about money. Your financial situation in divorce is the mark of how fair your divorce is, and it will determine how you will survive for the rest of your life or, at least, for some years to come. It affects you and it affects your children and other dependents.

A basic rule about the allocation of money in a divorce is that, when this issue walks in the door, decency, honor, fairness, empathy, and even truth fly out the window. Your husband, assuming he is the main wage earner, will want to hide, steal, deny, and secrete every dollar from you that he can. His lawyer and his employer may help him hide it from you. It doesn't matter about your needs or the children's needs or the fairness of the ultimate division. All that matters is money, because most men regard any money paid to an ex-wife as they would buying hay for a dead horse. They don't have the fun of frolicking in bed with you anymore.

I. SOME FACTS, TRICKS, AND UNSAVORY TRUTHS ABOUT THE MONEY

A. Manipulating Family Money

1. *Money can be physically hidden.* The first and obvious truth about money is that it can be physically hidden. Your husband can loot your joint bank accounts, for example, and bury the cash in a hole somewhere or put it in a bank account with only his name on it in another state or another country. Of course, if money is taken from a bank account, you will have knowledge that it was once there and your husband will have to account for it. The problem here is that by the time you have the bank statement showing the missing money, it is long gone.

2. *Money can be hidden in time.* Another way money can be hidden from you is for your husband to arrange that money due to him during marriage is deferred to a later date after he is divorced. If he can show that money was earned after separation, it will be his separate property. However, this is not always done in anticipation of a divorce and with the intent of cheating you, but it can have the same effect no matter what the motivation. For example, suppose husband makes a deal with his employer to defer paying a portion of his salary until later years when he retires. Initially, this may have been done to take advantage of income tax loopholes by postponing income until he is in a lower income tax bracket. However, it may have the effect of denying you a share in the money because it is payable after the divorce is final. Your attorney must learn about this and lay claim to

this deferred compensation as part of the marriage estate in which you should share.

3. *Money can be disguised.* Money can be disguised as something else and therefore not included in the marital property that you are supposed to share. You and your attorney have to be alert to penetrate the disguises and claim the property. For example, your husband may take money that is rightfully yours to share and put it in bank accounts under another name and over which he has sole control. The same thing is true of marital property—real estate, stocks, bonds, trust accounts—which could be put into front names, fictitious names, or company names. Yet your husband remains in sole control of them. Often these are part of the marital estate, and you need to find them.

4. *Money can be there without being there as money.* Your husband might be getting part of his pay in a form that is not money, but what money can buy. This is something that is often called "perks," payment in kind instead of payment in cash. For example, if your husband has the use of a car or apartment or vacation condo or golf club membership, that is all part of his compensation while he is married to you. Therefore, you have shared in it during marriage. These perks should be considered in setting support. You will need to recognize this kind of compensation and tell your lawyer about these perks. While as a nonemployee you will not receive a share of these, you can benefit from them by increasing the support payable to you by your husband.

5. *Credit can dry up.* One of the nastiest moves that your husband can make if you are not alert is that he can dry up your credit and make life difficult for you during the divorce and afterward. So often a woman's credit status is developed as part of her marital status. If you and your attorney are not vigilant, your husband might suddenly cancel all the charge accounts and credit cards held jointly in the family name. This will damage your credit, and you may not be in a position to obtain credit yourself. You, of course, could cancel all the same accounts or try to get them split into separate accounts while you are still married. However, as the nonemployed spouse, you may not be able to obtain credit on your record alone. A flip side to this is what some marriage partners do out of spite. They quickly run up the balances on all the charge and credit card accounts to burden the marriage with the higher debt, which lowers the amount of net

assets available to split in the final divorce settlement. It is a variation of stripping all the money out of joint bank accounts. Mean? Tricky? Yes, but often done in divorces.

B. Protecting Your Interests

Given the vindictiveness that often bubbles to the surface in divorce cases, it is important that you and your attorney move decisively and promptly to protect your financial interests. If you don't, your husband and his attorney will, and you'll be left out in the cold.

Since most of these protective measures take time to perfect, it underscores again the wisdom of keeping your plan to dissolve your marriage confidential at the beginning. Assuming that you finally decide to go ahead with the divorce, don't tell the children, friends, or other family members until you and your attorney have time to make your protective moves.

II. WHAT FINANCIAL RECORDS ARE IMPORTANT TO YOU

You must gather as much financial information about your marital property as possible. If you are not the primary wage earner, this will be more complicated than if you are. Or, perhaps wisely, you have been involved in the finances of the marriage all along and have ready access to the information. This information is key to protecting yourself and equipping your attorney to do a competent job for you. The checklist below can help guide you on what information you should try to collect.

FINANCIAL INFORMATION CHECKLIST

- Financial statements
- Income tax returns (plus W-2 forms and Kls)
- Canceled checks and bank statements
- Statements of stock accounts
- Copies of credit card and charge accounts
- Loan applications

CHECKLIST CONTINUED

- Employment contracts
- Work contracts for deferred pay and bonuses
- Details of payment for services rendered and of in-kind pay and payment vouchers
- Work expense account reports
- Details of pension, profit-sharing, and bonus plans
- Property received as gift or inheritance
- Professional licenses and degrees
- Special accounts: Keoghs, IRAs, etc.
- Detailed list of your separate property
- Trust funds or annuities present or future
- Income property
- Royalties, patents, and copyrights
- Real estate owned and mortgages against it
- Fine art
- Antiques, valuable collections

YOU'LL HATE TO DO THIS BUT WILL REGRET IT IF YOU DON'T

You will invest a lot of time and effort and some money gathering up all these records and documentation to prepare your attorney to give you strong representation. That will leave you so exhausted that you won't want to have them copied as protection against loss. This is a huge mistake! Copy all the material you have gathered and store it away in a waterproof, fireproof, insect-proof storage place that only you know about. Do not leave it with relatives or "friends." Sometimes as the divorce goes along these people may turn on you and give up your files to the other side.

III. PROTECTING YOUR FINANCIAL INTERESTS

A. Establishing Your Own Credit

As quietly as you can, and without arousing suspicion that you are planning a divorce, try to establish your own credit. Try to get credit card companies to issue you a card in your own name and have charge accounts established in your own name. If you have to explain why to the creditor, you can offer any number of plausible reasons, such as your desire to keep your charges separate from your husband's charges since he uses his cards and accounts largely for business; this will make the accounting and reimbursement of business expenses easier.

The point of doing this while you're married, particularly if you are unemployed or making less money than your husband, is that it is easier to obtain credit while you are married than when you are single, out of work, or in a low-paying job, or totally dependent upon support from your former spouse.

B. Keeping Your Assets Separate

Property you had before your marriage or have received as a separate gift or inheritance during your marriage is considered your sole and separate property unless you mix it into the marital property. For example, if you take money received as a gift or an inheritance and put it into your joint bank account, that generally makes it part of the marriage assets and not yours alone. If you hold real estate and stocks and bonds that you had before marriage or received as a gift or inheritance in your separate name, it is probably your separate property. If you put it in both your names, it becomes part of the marital assets in most cases. Thus, it is extremely important that you maintain your separate assets in your name only. There is *never* any reason to add your husband's name to your separate accounts, and if you have done so, you may try to reestablish your separate property by again setting up separate bank accounts.

WORD OF CAUTION

When your husband learns of the divorce, you can expect him to try to strip your joint accounts, hide personal property, bury his assets, and make all the protective moves that you might be making, too. Don't be surprised, just be first!

Beyond that, you should make up a list and identify all the property that you can legitimately claim is your separate property. This should be more than just a list. Itemize the location of these separate assets, give identifying information such as certificate numbers in the case of stock and the facts to establish the separate nature of your property.

C. Keeping Careful Inventories and Accountings

You may also want to have other separate accounts to put your share of marital money in, such as your salary after separation, or money you remove for safekeeping from the joint account. Your husband will claim his share of that down the line as you go through the divorce settlement, but you will have control of it at a time when you may need to have control of some money. Whatever you do with the marital money and other assets, carefully document your moves, because you will have to account for it later when it is time to settle up between you.

For example, if you have a joint safe-deposit box, at the very least you should open it and check the contents. Even if you don't remove anything, it is important for you to make an inventory of what is in the box. Even better, you should have a disinterested party make an inventory of what is in the box and give you and your lawyer an affidavit of what is there at the date of separation. You should do the same thing with collections, fine art, antiques, and whatever other valuables you both have. There are, for example, firms that take videotapes of the contents of homes and maintain a videotape file in case an inventory of your personal belongings is needed for insurance purposes. If there is such a service in your town, this would be a good time to use it. If there isn't such a service, perhaps your local camera store has someone who could do it for you and attest that it's an accurate video of what was in the house. You might want them to also include in the tape a close-up video shot of the current newspaper to establish the date that it was taken. You can take your own pictures of the contents of your home using a throw-away camera, easily purchased at a drugstore.

Why all this monitoring of your marital assets by disinterested third parties? Because, sad to say, when the divorce comes out in the open, both husband and wife too often will accuse the other of stealing and hiding family assets. When that occurs, if you can establish an accurate and independently made inventory of family assets, it will give you several advantages. First, it will refute claims that you have acted in bad faith and tried to steal any of the marital property. Second, it will impress the judge with your honesty and careful attention to details. This impression can carry over to other aspects of the negotiations that will work in your favor. Finally, it will stun the opposition to realize that you are so carefully prepared, and they will understand that you are going to be a formidable opponent. This can give you and your attorney a psychological edge in the proceedings.

D. Paying Off Some Bills

In most states, the debts that either husband or wife incur during the period of the marriage are the joint debts of the marriage, so it is often a smart move to pay off a number of the debts you have while still married. You will have to pay the debts eventually, and paying them out of joint funds may give you some advantage over paying them out of your own funds after the divorce. One of the issues will be the termination date of the marriage. In some states the marriage may end at the date of separation and in others at the date the judgment dissolving the marriage is entered. Often liability for debts incurred at or about the time of the separation will depend on the type of debt incurred. If it was for food or rent, necessities of life for the parties, it generally will be a joint debt. If it is for a new fishing pole to feed your husband's passion for fishing, it probably will be considered a separate debt, and he will be confirmed that debt in the settlement or judgment.

E. Notification of Creditors

To protect yourself against the tactic we mentioned earlier of the opposing side running up big bills on credit cards and charge accounts, you will want to notify all your creditors when you are ready to go public with the divorce action that you are no longer responsible for your husband's debts. Often a notice is also run in the newspaper; your attorney will know what the proper legal way to do this is and what the custom is in your area.

IV. FINDING THE MONEY HE'S HIDING FROM YOU

As cynical as it sounds, the temptation for your husband to try to cheat you out of your fair share of the marriage assets is almost always too great for him to resist. If there is some way he can defer income, conceal assets, flimflam you, he will probably do it. It usually requires a sainted man to resist the chance to deny you money or assets, and if he were such a sainted man, the chances are you wouldn't be getting a divorce. He feels rejected and abandoned if you are leaving him, and if he's leaving you—usually for another woman—he needs all the money he can get to woo and impress the other woman just as he once did you.

If you doubt that your husband will hide assets from you, consider this: The Internal Revenue Service estimates that U.S. taxpayers—mostly men—conceal some $200 *billion* from the IRS every year. Such conduct may result in a long jail term. What does hiding assets from *you* carry as a penalty? Essentially nothing.

How will you embark on a treasure hunt to find out where the money is? Even if you are a major wage earner or the principal wage earner, the chances are he is going to try to hold out on you when it comes to negotiating a settlement. You can hire a private detective to determine this information, but think a minute. You are the person who actually knows your husband—you know his routines, his habits—and you probably will have an easier time collecting clues and checking out those clues than would a private detective. So you may want to do at least some of this sleuthing yourself. Some of this is as simple as checking official records or known directories or computer databases. Find all personal papers around the house, in storage, or in safe-deposit boxes. These clues often will lead you in the direction of a hidden asset or account. Watch for bank deposit slips on banks whose names are unfamiliar to you. Look for matchbook covers, which, even in this modern no-smoking era, people still manage to collect.

Here are some of the places that you want to check for assets your husband might have concealed:

A. Direct Checks

1. *Secret bank accounts.* These are not necessarily secret, they are just secret from you. There are national database services to check on bank accounts in your husband's name in banks around the country. Some of these can also research certain overseas banks, although this is much more difficult.

2. *Property held separately.* Sometimes your husband will invest marital money in real estate in his own name, and unless he tells you about it or the property tax bill comes to the house, you won't know anything about it. One quick way to check this is by scanning the taxpayer rolls on file at the county recorder's office. Or, check the county recorder's taxpayer rolls in the county where you have other property or where he goes on business or where you own a second home together. People tend not to invest in real estate they have never seen or are not familiar with, so think back to that unexpected trip to the lake country or to the shore.

3. *Rare property, fine art, and collections.* He might have sunk money into some rare items, fine art, or a valuable collection of stamps, coins, figurines, and so on. Sometimes there are societies of collectors that issue directories of their collections, and if your husband is known to have a sharp interest in paintings or stamps or miniature toy soldiers, check for your husband's name in such a directory or catalog.

4. *Phony tricks.* A device used in a variety of forms to hide money from a wife getting a divorce is the phony document. If you and your husband have, for whatever reason, been filing separate income tax returns, or have filed a joint return that you have never carefully scrutinized before signing it, don't be surprised if your husband or

his creative accountant use the opportunity presented by a divorce to create phony documents, even tax returns, to demonstrate a different financial picture from what is actually the case.

Your husband may go so far as to obligate himself for a loan that is nothing more than a ploy to create debt where there is none. Be aware of the backdated promissory note for a "loan" made to the married couple by a friend or a business associate that you have never heard of until the divorce comes along. The amount of this "loan" diminishes the net assets of the marriage subject to division between husband and wife. After the divorce is over, the bogus note between friends is torn up over a beer and the wife is cheated out of her fair share of marital assets.

5. *Children's or relatives' bank accounts.* Another way of burying money is to slip it over time into bank accounts, trust accounts, escrow accounts in the names of the children or of a trusted relative. While these accounts are in someone else's name, the terms of the account may give your husband absolute control over them, and unless you are aware of these funds, they may not be included in the accounting of the assets of your marriage. You may not feel that you want a share of these assets, but you need to know about them to assure that they will be kept and used for the designated beneficiary.

6. *Undervalued assets.* One very common way for husbands to minimize the joint assets is to undervalue the marital assets over which they have management and control on their financial statements. For example, suppose joint funds have been invested in real estate or fine art, jewelry, antiques, or collectibles. Your husband will want to undervalue those assets he expects to receive in the division of property and overvalue those he expects you will receive. He would, then, want to undervalue his antique car or stamp collection and overvalue your jewelry. (Often jewelry, if given on birthdays or holidays, is truly a gift and should be considered your separate property. Keep all notes of gifts and dated receipts.) The cleverness of this is that the asset is not physically hidden. It is out in the open and the existence of it is acknowledged, but its *true value* is hidden. That is a tactic you must prepare for by having the assets appraised by independent appraisers.

One method of undervaluing an asset is perfectly legal under tax laws, but it can rob you of your fair share of the marriage estate. That is by using the depreciated value of an asset in dividing your property. Depreciation is a deduction made on books and records from the value of certain income-producing assets, such as improved real estate and equipment. Even automobiles used in a business can be depreciated. The theory is that machinery and buildings (you cannot depreciate the land under your buildings) wear out in time and have to be replaced. The simplest way of figuring out how much value such an asset loses each year is to divide the value of it when new by the number of years it will last; the IRS has charts and tables for those calculations. Suppose you and your husband own a rental unit that was worth $100,000 new and it has a useful life of twenty-five years. Over those twenty-five years it will depreciate or lose its original value at the rate of $4,000 a year. ($100,000 ÷ 25 = $4,000.) This is called the straight-line method of depreciation.

However, the IRS allows one to determine depreciation at least two other ways, which have the effect of writing down the value of the building much faster—in one case almost twice as fast. The bigger the deduction from the value of the building, the lower the income taxes you will have to pay in the early years of owning that income property, since depreciation is considered to be a business expense. That's the good news when you are still married, but the bad news is that your husband might claim that the asset is only worth its depreciated value when the time arrives to divide the property in the divorce settlement negotiation. In fact, the depreciated value of many properties has little relationship to the market value of the asset. So you need to watch for these kinds of tricks that undervalue the assets of the marriage—particularly those assets your husband wants confirmed to him after the divorce.

7. *The Chapter 11 scam.* If your husband is in business, he may decide to pull the Chapter 11 bankruptcy scam when he sees a divorce looming up. In days not so long gone, going into bankruptcy was a disgrace. Now it is a very common business strategy to stall creditors, reorganize your financial existence, and protect the businessman from financial pressures. Some of the biggest companies in America today have declared Chapter 11 bankruptcy, and they are still doing business every day! So if your husband does that, don't pull out the hankie to wipe away your tears of sympathy. Call your lawyer instead and get a good accountant on the job to confirm the truth about your husband's business or personal financial condition. Don't be fooled or intimidated by the Chapter 11 scam.

8. *The Hollywood accounting gimmick.* Even without the bankruptcy scam, a careful study of your husband's financial statements and reports, both personal and business, is a wise investment. Hollywood studios, for example, are notorious for their "creative accounting." This "creative accounting" has them spending $15 million to make a movie that brings in $100 million but that still, according to their financial accounting, loses money. What actually has happened is that personal expenses may have been run through the business accounts: limousine bills, mortgage payments, vacations, wardrobe, to say nothing of restaurant and catering charges. This type of accounting is endemic in business accounting in some closely held or solely owned companies, and your husband's firm may be one of those which uses such creative accounting.

9. *Skimming cash and off-the-books cash.* Many businesses do a big cash business, and this offers many opportunities to skim cash that is not recorded in the company's books and records. If your husband has such a business or works in such a business, there is a chance that he may be pocketing money that is not reported to the tax authorities or, perhaps, not to his boss and, certainly, not to you.

Here are just a few examples of how that works that you should be aware of so you can make your claim against hidden assets. If he is a bartender or food service businessman, or is in a position to control the cash billed and paid, he can collect cash for what he dispenses and put only part of it in the cash register. For example, a fifth of whiskey will normally hold twenty-four one-ounce shots or drinks. If the bartender only collects for twenty-two shots, the owner may assume that the other two shots are lost due to spillage or evaporation. In fact, the bartender may simply be pocketing the money for those two drinks himself. The famous former madam in the San Francisco Bay area, Sally Stanford, understood this kind of skimming and used to measure the whiskey in her bottles behind the bar with a ruler at the beginning of every shift to make sure her bartenders weren't skimming to reduce her income.

Cash registers were invented to keep a record of all the money taken in at a business to protect the owner or, possibly, to provide a record for the tax man. It has a printed tape or electronic computer, and in order to open the cash drawer a sale must be rung. However, a common trick is for the person at the cash register to ring up one sale and leave the drawer open and make change for the next sale or two without ringing it up. At the end of the shift, there is much more money in the drawer than the record shows, and that difference is pocketed either by the owner or employee or whoever is doing the open-drawer trick.

Joe Mullen, a famous New York City private detective, encountered a slightly more sophisticated variation of the open-drawer trick. He was called in to solve the case of somebody skimming money from a well-known Manhattan restaurant. He sent undercover agents into the place night after night to see if they could detect what was going wrong. Every night they turned in written reports saying that every sale was rung up on one of the five cash registers and they could not detect any irregularities. After reading these reports, Mullen figured it out. He called the owner and asked him how many cash registers he had in the restaurant, and the owner answered, "Four." The manager had put his own cash register in the place and pocketed all the money rung up on that.

So what is the point of all this? What does it have to do with your divorce and your husband hiding money from you? These are all illustrations of how your husband could be skimming money that he's reporting to no one and hiding from you. The range of such ideas is unlimited and do not always involve a cash register.

B. Telltale Clues

In addition to obvious evidence that your husband is hiding assets such as the existence of heretofore unknown bank accounts or property held in his name alone, there are many other clues that should set you on the path of discovery.

1. *Insurance polices or premium receipts.* Check what these policies or the policies relating to the premium receipts insure. Is there insurance for damage or loss to fine art or collections or property that you didn't know about?

2. *Canceled checks and charge card receipts.* Canceled checks and charge card receipts should be carefully reviewed to make sure you understand every charge and every payment. If there are payments to payees who are unfamiliar to you, find out the purpose of the payment. Take time to check it out. You might discover funds going into a secret bank account or investment account, or it might be a mort-

gage payment or rent on a safe-deposit box or storage unit that you know nothing about and that contains assets that belong to you.

3. *Business books and accounts.* If your husband is in business for himself, he has a wide range of opportunities to hide assets from you. Your accountant must carefully examine and understand the books and records of the business. Your husband will have the opportunity to bury enormous amounts of money in payments to suppliers, contractors, workers, and so on from whom he may be getting kickbacks, discounts, and bonuses that he is salting away without your knowing about it. Getting a look at his business books without arousing his suspicions may be difficult, and you and your attorney may have to subpoena them after the divorce has been filed, but it is very important that you examine them very carefully and understand the sources and disposition of funds in and out of the business. And always remember that most clever businessmen keep three sets of books: one for the IRS, one for the partner, and one for themselves.

4. *Codes.* Nobody can keep everything in their head, and if your husband is stealing and hiding assets from the marriage and from you, he probably has some system of keeping track of what he has carefully and systematically taken out of the joint assets. A common device is for him to invent some kind of short code that he can keep in his daily calendar or diary or on the check stubs or in a drawer or safe-deposit box or wherever. The point is that if you find cryptic notations that you don't understand, hold on to them or make copies of them. Don't throw them away until you or your attorney or accountant can determine what they mean. Even if you never figure out what the code means, revealing to your husband at a divorce settlement agreement that you have the code, and that he will be questioned about it, could make him anxious to make a quicker and more generous settlement

5. *Computer files.* More and more records are kept in computers and on computer disks. It is essential that you obtain access to your husband's personal computer files and disks so that you or some one else can understand what is in those files. This can give you clues to hidden assets, and since computerized stock and bank account management is now growing common, it can reveal hidden stock accounts, bank accounts, and a variety of information about assets that he is trying to keep secret from you.

6. *Faked travel and entertainment expenses.* Carefully check supposed entertainment and travel expenses against your husband's calendar and records. If he is claiming travel or entertainment expenses when you knew he was home or someplace else, you should know about it. Where did the money from those phony expense claims go? In some executive watering holes in Manhattan and Los Angeles, we personally know of executives who tip waiters well for running several charge slips through at one time using the executive's credit card. One of those slips is used to pay for the meal and the others—conveniently blank except for the restaurant's imprint and the executive's credit card imprint—leave in the executive's pocket. These are later filled out for different dates at which alleged business entertainment was done for which the executive is reimbursed. Where does that money go? You need to find out because, even if it is ill-gotten money, you may profit from your knowledge of this tactic in the divorce.

7. *Gifts and goodies.* If one of the reasons you want a divorce is because your husband has been busy having an affair or two, you need to check out his girlfriend's lifestyle and see if he is providing her with such gifts and goodies as rent money, clothes, furs, jewelry, vacations, or cars. Is she living rent-free in jointly owned property? Find out as much about these misappropriations of your assets as possible; try to locate where he is buying these gifts and goodies. If he is paying cash, that's a sign that he has a trove of money somewhere that he doesn't want traced through the paper trail of checks and receipts.

C. Unbelievable But True Tricks

When the love is gone and you are in the throes of divorce, you may be dealing with a desperate or daring husband. People (men *and* women) do insane things all the time, so be prepared for the strange, unexpected, or dangerous in this sensitive time in your lives. Here are some of the things husbands have actually done to deal with a wife who is divorcing them or to whom they are informed they may have to pay support or with whom they must share their property:

1. *Murder.* There are thousands of cases over the years of husbands who have murdered their wives or arranged the murder of their wives in order to be rid of the marriage and keep the marital assets.

The newspaper accounts of such conduct are widespread. The important thing is to be aware that bizarre and threatening situations can arise in the course of a separation and divorce; be alert and protect yourself.

2. *Faked deaths or disappearances.* There are, likewise, many cases of husbands who will overnight raid the assets, then fake their own murder or simply disappear. If they disappear, your marital assets could disappear with them or be so entangled that you will need a attorney to sort out your legal position. In some states, the missing husband has to have been gone for a specific length of time before he can be declared dead so you can claim his life insurance and share of the family assets. In the meantime, your life could be in limbo and you may face difficult times. Obviously, in these extreme cases you will wish you had armed yourself with knowledge of the joint assets.

It is not easy to protect yourself against a husband who is so vindictive that he would simply disappear. But you can protect your joint assets and preclude his taking assets with him. Judges will issue temporary and then permanent restraining orders against the holders of the funds, banks and stock brokerage houses. If your husband can't get his hands on a lot of assets quickly, he is less likely to resort to some of these extreme schemes.

CHAPTER NINE

After You File for Divorce

IN THIS CHAPTER YOU WILL:

> I. Review the divorce process and your interim problems.
> II. Learn some important words and concepts.
> III. Learn what you shouldn't do pending your divorce.

The closest thing to purgatory that most people will endure in their lifetime is that period between the filing of a divorce action and the awarding of the final divorce decree. Most people going through a divorce have to deal with at least three major crises at this same time:

1. The emotional crisis of breaking up a relationship.
2. A financial crisis.
3. A struggle over custody of children.

Any one of these crises would be enough to turn hair white, grab the pit of the stomach, and make you want to throw up every morning, but you are enduring three of them. It is no wonder that you feel that life is crazy some days. We and your attorney will try to help you through all these crises with information and some guidance.

When people die, it is sometimes said in mitigation of their death that at least they went painlessly and quickly. When a marriage dies, the process is neither painless nor quick. Our purpose is to try to help ease you through it with learning in advance what to expect and how you can prepare yourself for the ordeal.

I. THE STEPS TO FREEDOM

This chapter is about the interim period between filing for divorce and the granting of a judgment of dissolution or divorce. However, to put it into a time and task perspective, let's briefly review again the steps involved in obtaining your divorce. We have mentioned some of them before and will expand on most of them later; here is an overview so you can see the road map you will follow to obtain your freedom from the marriage that died.

A. When the Marriage Ends

You or your husband decide that you cannot continue being married to each other. You both have changed, and each of you needs to get on with his and her life. The moment you decide to divorce is when the process really begins. As one attorney put it, it is the season that the marriage ends and the hating begins. Sad and pathetic, but too often true.

As we noted before, you have basically three choices after you have decided the marriage is over and you can't live together any longer.

1. *Walk.* One or both of you can simply walk out and start a new life. This leaves many issues legally unresolved that may come back to haunt you and inhibit your new life. Simply walking out is not something we recommend, even through we know that thousands of people in the United States do exactly that every year. They walk out

the door, ostensibly to get something at the grocery store and they are never seen again.

2. *Legal separation.* Another choice is to remain legally married but not living together. This has a certain appeal but a number of pitfalls, because of your continued attachment to a spouse whom you no longer love and whom you can no longer trust.

3. *Divorce or dissolution.* Finally, there is the option of choice for most people, splitting up the assets of the marriage and going your separate ways: divorce, or as it is called in some states, dissolution of marriage.

B. Separation or Divorce?

Your lawyer will prepare the official papers for you to sign and file with the court, petitioning for a decree of legal separation or divorce and seeking orders for division of property, support, custody and visitation, and attorney fees.

Whether you decide on separation or divorce, and the vast majority choose divorce, you and your spouse will have to come to two different kinds of settlements. One of these settlements is the final, permanent settlement between you governing the division of property and custody of children. (If you have children, for their sake you will continue to have some kind of relationship with your ex-husband, so that, too, will begin with the final settlement.)

However, the permanent settlement will usually take some weeks or even months or years to hammer out, and in the meantime you need to have a temporary arrangement to cover the details of day-to-day living pending the final divorce.

C. Temporary Arrangements

Until the final settlement is agreed to or until the unresolved issues between you are settled in court, the two of you need to enter into a mutually acceptable temporary arrangement. However, do not do this lightly; insist on every major point that is important to you because temporary settlement arrangements often set a precedent for the permanent settlement. Here is a checklist to help you outline the terms of the temporary settlement that are satisfactory to you.

TEMPORARY ARRANGEMENTS CHECKLIST

Financial responsibilities
    Alimony—amount and length of time
    Payment of past and future bills
    Insurance premiums
    Income tax obligations
    Child support—amount and length of time
    Special support arrangements including school expenses
    Housing
Other responsibilities
    Protection of dependents
    Health care of children and pets
    Maintenance of assets
    Maintenance of insurance, funds, etc.
    Memberships
    Visitation with children
    Protection against violence and slander
    Public statements
Emergencies
    Is a "stay-away" order needed?
    Penalties for violation of court orders
    Nonviolent emergencies

D. Preparing for Emergencies

There are emergencies that will probably arise during the interim period while your divorce is pending. Due to the very nature of emergencies it is difficult to anticipate all such events, but some mechanism must be put in place to cope with emergencies during the period of separation.

Emergencies during this time generally fall into one of three categories: money, violence, and children.

1. *Money.* To emphasize the point, we tell you again that your husband may attempt to loot marital funds out of joint accounts, run up bills on charge accounts, take property out of the house, threaten to stop making payments on mortgages, charge accounts, and so on. He is angry, vengeful, and punitive. He wants to punish you for aban-

doning him, for not putting up with his misbehavior, or he may want to make you so destitute that you will be forced to return to him.

None of this will work, of course, if you have followed our earlier instructions in this book or if you are the principal wage earner in the family, because you will have moved first and protected yourself as we told you how to do, or because you have your own money. However, if you haven't followed our suggestions—and many women don't because they cannot believe that their husband will do all the things that we have described—your attorney will need to obtain a court order spelling out the temporary financial arrangements during this period.

This would include:
a. Temporary support for you and children
b. Payment of marital bills (within limits)
c. Payment of mortgage on and upkeep of home
d. Restraints against bleeding marital assets
e. Restraints against stealing or hiding marital property

2. *Violence.* Even without the tawdry tabloid tales of O.J. Simpson, James Caan, and others, every woman in America who hasn't been living in a cave knows that one out of five women is regularly battered by the man who supposedly loves her. Even if your husband isn't one of those yet, you can never be sure what might take him over the edge.

This is a book about the law, and we would be remiss to you if we weren't straight about domestic violence and the law. There are court orders, "stay-away" orders, restraining orders, and the like that will require your husband to leave you alone, stay away from you and the house, not go near your place of employment, the children, and on and on into the night, and your lawyer knows how to get them. Despite that, there is no guarantee that an angry, frenzied, or drunken man won't ignore all the orders you obtain, batter down your door, and beat the hell out of you. The reality is that neither the court nor your attorney, nor the police, nor the U.S. Marines can protect you entirely. You have to protect yourself as much as you can.

Some of the ways you can protect yourself are spelled out in a later chapter, as well as in books on self-protection, and we urge you to study them carefully. The danger of physical violence against you or your children or relatives is very real and very serious. There are too many women who wait too long to protect themselves and their loved ones from an irrational and violent husband, ex-husband, or lover. They end up not being able to dial 911 because they are dead or injured.

3. Children. Naturally, the children can be a major pawn in the fight between estranged husband and wife. It is a sad commentary that the fight for custody of the children often has more to do with vengeance and hurting the other partner than it has to do with concern over the welfare of the kids.

You need to worry about the possibility that your husband may grab the children from school or home or relatives and take them to another state or another country and hide them from you before a lawsuit is even filed and restraining orders and custody orders can be obtained. In these instances, the legal problems and costs of trying to get them back from another state or, particularly, another country are difficult and expensive. You don't want to have to do it if you can, in the first instance, avoid his grabbing the kids and taking off.

Thus, when considering divorce, it is wise to attempt to obtain orders for temporary custody and restraints against removal of the children on an *ex parte* basis without informing your husband until the orders are served on him. In order to do that you will have to have some evidence that he is likely to remove the children, such as threats to do so in the past. Here again there are the usual court orders, which your lawyer can assist you in obtaining, that will forbid him from snatching the kids and that, you hope, he will obey.

All of this business about court orders is made even more depressing when you realize what usually happens if you call 911 and are successful in getting your husband arrested for violating a court order. The reality is that, unless he has a record of arrests and convictions for violent crimes—which is relatively unlikely—he may be let off with a warning and a modest fine. Or even if he has done something serious to you, he could be "diverted" by the court.

Our legal and criminal system is so overburdened that various states have tried to find ways of easing the load on jails and officials by keeping offenders with minor crimes on their record out of prison. And in many jurisdictions, wife beating is still considered more of a family affair. Regardless of the fact that your spouse may have punched you in the face and slammed you around, our system would probably still classify the crime as minor and try to divert your husband. This may put him into a rehabilitation program, and in exchange for his promise never to do it again the system lets him back on the street where he can intimidate and threaten you again. No, it's not a pretty situation, and we want you to understand what you may face so you can be ready and can protect yourself.

E. Negotiation or Mediation?

The issues in dissolving your marriage will have to be settled by some procedure in order for you to secure a legal separation or divorce. Working backward, the most complicated and expensive way of settling the issues is through a court trial. Court trials are expensive because they often involve a substantial amount of waiting time, during which you and your lawyer sit for hours in a corridor outside the courtroom, with your lawyer's meter running all that time at $150 to $350 or more an hour. Because there aren't enough judges and courts to handle the tremendous trial load in a timely way, alternatives to the court system have evolved. As a result, over 95 percent of divorce cases in this country are settled before going to court, and the judge essentially just formalizes the settlement worked out between the two sides in advance.

Laura Mansnerus, writing in the *New York Times* in June of 1994, praised the new trend in choosing the mediation process versus dueling lawyers. She said that mediation was becoming more and more popular because it was cheaper, there was less rancor, and it settled things more quickly. She said, "For twenty years enthusiasts of mediation have insisted that techniques developed in labor law can make for better divorces. Bringing a couple before a single disinterested party, they say, yields settlement with less expense and rancor than having two lawyers hash it out."

Members of the Academy of Family Mediators claim that the typical mediated divorce can be settled for about $5,000, while the typical conventional adversarial system pitting two lawyers on behalf of their clients will be three to four times that much.

There is much in what the fans of mediation say, but there are some *serious pitfalls* for you in what they don't say. Generally speaking, we don't think mediation is suitable in *most* divorce settlements for several good reasons and for one major, unrecognized reason that can hurt you if you miss it.

THE SECRET FAILING OF MEDIATION

The object of mediation is to have a third party sit with husband and wife and hammer out an agreement. The secret failing of this is that the objective is getting both of you make an agreement—not to get a settlement that's fair for you. The goal is a deal—not necessarily a *fair deal*—just a deal.

There are other weakness to mediation that you should know about, and when you read the next paragraph, we think you'll agree with us that a settlement negotiated by lawyers representing each of you is the surest way you will secure a fair deal.

The other shortcomings of mediation include:

- Mediators often are not licensed, regulated or particularly trained in the law in many states. It is a real mistake to put your matter in the hands of a mediator who has no legal training. Divorce laws are complex and require complete understanding by the mediator.
- Mediators don't represent the best interests of either side. Their goal is compromise so a bargain can be made, but there are things about which it isn't wise or fair for you to bargain, such as custody or protection against abuse or a fair cut of the family estate.
- Because the mediator, even if he or she is a licensed attorney, does not actually represent either one of you, the attorney-client privilege that keeps everything you tell him or her secret may not apply.
- Mediation does not guarantee that you are getting your husband to reveal all the details of his net worth, his business, his hidden assets, and so on. Without that information, you can be sure you will be shortchanged in the money department. In mediation you often forgo formal discovery. This may be detrimental to you as the spouse who does not manage and is not in control of the assets.

- Finally, even when the mediation is complete and a deal has been struck, the agreement still has to be drawn up by a licensed attorney for presentation to the court, so what is the point? That attorney should be with you throughout the mediation.

F. Settlement or Not?

As we have suggested above, the best way to settle the issues between you and your husband is probably through a settlement conference or conferences between his attorney and yours. This, as we have said, is done in over 95 percent of the family law cases. Whether or not you are present or your husband is present is part of the strategy that you and your attorney need to work out.

SPECIAL SETTLEMENT SECRET

If you want to succeed at the settlement conference, put yourself in your husband's shoes and do the same preparation: make up what you believe will be your husband's priority list and temporary budget. Debate them with your attorney against your lists so you can anticipate which way negotiations might go even before they actually start.

If you use the settlement approach, there are several things you must do with your attorney to prepare. The most important aspects necessary to come to a settlement is that you begin the negotiations at the right time in the divorce process and that you are ready—that you and your attorney know everything you need to know to make intelligent decisions about settlement of the various issues.

1. *Set your list of priorities.* As we have noted elsewhere, your attorney and you need to establish a set of priorities for negotiating a settlement. Remember the categories of Must Have, Like to Have, and Don't Care.

Your attorney must be a good negotiator, so armed with a detailed list of your priorities that she can properly negotiate the settlement you can live with. It probably will not match your priority list exactly, but there is much to be gained through negotiation. What can't be settled through negotiation will have to be decided by the judge.

2. *Give your attorney power to do what has to be done.* You must do more than hire an attorney to represent you and to negotiate the divorce settlement for you, you must psychologically support and encourage that attorney. You must accept her guidance on the strategy and tactics to be followed—not without question because she must be willing to explain things to you—with confidence. Remember this is probably your first divorce negotiation and it may be her five-hundredth. If your attorney doesn't have your full backing and support, she can't do a good job for you. Do not be lazy. Do your own homework to assist your attorney in representing you. Go through financial records. Find out how much you paid over the last few years on each toy and towel. Work hard in your divorce.

TEMPORARY LIVING EXPENSES BUDGET CHECKLIST (FOR YOU AND YOUR DEPENDENTS)

Food (in house and out)
Maintaining the home
    Monthly mortgage or rent
    Taxes
    Insurance on house and furniture
    Utilities
    Yard care and other maintenance
    Building, furniture, and appliance upkeep
    Security
Clothing
Medical, dental, and therapy expenses
Insurance on self, children, and car
Transportation costs (gas, car payment, etc.)
Personal expenses (grooming, haircuts, etc.)
Recreation
Gifts and contributions

CHECKLIST CONTINUED

Household expenses (dry cleaning, newspapers, etc.)
Education expense for children (books, etc.)
Savings
Taxes on income

---

3. *Work up a credible temporary budget for yourself.*

4. *Honestly confront the emergencies you may face.* Realistically face the problems you have had with your husband and evaluate what protections you need from the ways in which he may try to harm you or the children physically or financially. Inform your attorney frankly about these dangers and insist on obtaining appropriate protective orders from the court.

As we said earlier, the courts and the police have realistic limits on how effective and timely their protection of you and the children can be, but you must get the appropriate court orders anyhow. It gives you a basis from which to build your protection, and it gives the police the right to act to protect you even if after the fact. It is not perfect and it is not complete, but it will help. And the fact is that most husbands obey court orders because they don't want to jeopardize their jobs or the balance of their lives by being arrested or imprisoned.

G. Going Back

Speaking of being realistic, you must be realistic about the possibility of reconciliation. Whatever you felt the night you decided to go ahead with the divorce, or the day you hired your attorney, or the day the legal action was actually filed with the court, there is always the chance that you won't go through with the divorce.

People do change their minds, and you and your husband might reconcile. In fact, some women will go to the length of filing a divorce just to frighten their husband into giving up an affair and returning to home and hearth. Both of you may become exhausted over the battle and find yourselves unwilling to go through the pain and the business of hurting each other, so you get back together. Or, through marriage counseling with a therapist or members of the family or friends, you persuade yourself and each other to stay married. In most states you can halt the divorce proceedings at any point before the final decree is entered. You will still be on the hook for legal fees, court costs, and so on, but you can call the divorce quits instead of calling the marriage quits.

II. GUIDE TO IMPORTANT TERMS AND LANGUAGE

Words can confuse and deceive all of us, and you may be at a disadvantage in a legal morass because there are some technical words you should know in order to understand properly what is going on. We have a comprehensive list of divorce-case words and their meaning at the back of the book, but here we just mention a few you need to know at this point in the divorce process.

Contested and *uncontested*. A *contested* case is where the other side fights you. An *uncontested* case is where either the other side doesn't fight or both sides agree. Most divorces start out contested, but through negotiation and pretrial settlements, they end up uncontested. If the other side doesn't even show up, it is called a default in your favor.

Complaint or *petition, summons* and *answer* or *response.* The document your lawyer files for you saying you want a divorce is called the *complaint,* or in some states, a *petition.* Your husband is sent a copy of the complaint or petition and is called on to reply to it. The *summons* or a copy of it accompanies the complaint or petition. The summons is the official court process requiring your husband to respond to the complaint or petition. When his lawyer sends your lawyer and the court his reply, that is called the *answer* or the *response.*

Petition. A *petition* or application can also be a request you or your husband makes to the judge and the court during the pendency of the proceeding. You might petition the court for temporary alimony and child support, a stay-away order or temporary custody of the children, for example. This is also called *Order to Show Cause.*

Orders. Orders are just what they sound like, the demands and instructions of the judge to both you and your husband about what you can do and not do.

Ex parte. These are special court orders often given before a hearing on a particular question and without notifying the other side, although in most cases the court requires some notification prior to ruling on the *ex parte* application. They are issued in special situations where the court must move quickly. For example, the court could issue an ex parte order forbidding your husband from selling any of your joint property. After the ex parte order is issued, your husband would be notified that the court has issued the order and set a date when he can come to a hearing to dispute the order, but in the meantime the order is in effect. An ex parte application usually requires a showing of some emergency situation requiring the issuance of the order without a hearing.

With prejudice and *without prejudice.* A court order issued *with prejudice* means that the order cannot be changed unless either side can produce evidence that the circumstances that prompted the order have changed significantly. *Without prejudice* means that the order can be changed anytime after a hearing without showing any particular change in the circumstances.

Spousal support or *alimony.* Monthly support payments from one spouse to the other. The terms are used interchangeably, as are the terms *divorce* and *dissolution*.

Well, those are enough new words and phrases for you for the moment. We look at more of these in appropriate places in other chapters.

III. BEHAVIOR DURING THE PRELIMINARY PERIOD

During the time you are in limbo between being married and living with your husband, and the time the final decree is issued, you need to be circumspect in your behavior. If you are not, it could create repercussions in your case and cause you trouble and expense. Some, but not all, of the sensitive areas of behavior include these:

A. Dating

Again, let us caution you that during this period you may be lonely and vulnerable, but it is advisable not to become heavily involved in dating right away. Not only will your dating become a subject, however irrelevant, in the divorce, but the stress of beginning a new re-lationship during the period of separation will not be conducive to easing mental strain. We suggest your social activities during separation be confined to dates with groups of friends. Don't pair off with a man, and try to attend only innocuous events such as mainstream movies, art galleries, or the theater.

You can assume that, if your husband wants to fight you aggressively in the divorce using the kids as a lever, and wants to keep you from getting any money, he will have you followed, photographed, and tape-recorded. He might even hire someone to seduce you into a sexual escapade or other inappropriate activities. How, for example, would your custody case go if your husband could produce tapes, photos, and recordings of you cavorting in the nude with three men and a goat? Or snorting lines of cocaine? You get the point.

Forget about the sex and concentrate on what is *really* important, the money. If you plan to take a live-in lover to soften your bitter loneliness and provide solace during those long, cold nights, don't do it. If your husband finds out you are living with another man during this time, he has a great case for not paying you any temporary support or permanent alimony. Anytime you have to choose between a few minutes of hot sex or a lifetime of cold cash, follow the Woody Allen rule: "Take the money and run."

B. Having Sex with Your Estranged Husband

Avoid having sex with your attorney (we have mentioned that a number of times and advisedly so) or your estranged husband. For example, in states that require a waiting period for the divorce to become final, having sex with the man you're technically still married to, while claiming you can't stand him and want to be free, may convince the court you aren't serious and the time you have already waited may be nullified, causing you to begin the process again.

C. Avoiding Physical or Emotional Violence

Remember, you may hate this man, possibly you even have reason to fear him: keep away from him. Don't try stupid revenge tactics such as following him when he is dating other women, deflating his tires, or smashing his car windows. Don't play telephone harassment games because these calls can be traced back to you and result in criminal prosecution by the telephone company. Of course, telephone harassment games also show your immaturity and inability to confront the real issues.

There are many cases where divorced wives and husbands engage in irrational behavior. In the tragic Broderick case, Elisabeth Broderick began the nightmare by leaving obscene messages on her estranged husband's telephone answering machine and one day drove her car through his front door into the living room. Judges take such behavior to mean you are too emotionally and mentally unstable and untrustworthy to have custody of the children or much of anything else. Elisabeth and her estranged husband, Dan, ultimately were divorced, and he got the kids and most of the money. Elisabeth later sneaked into Dan's bedroom and murdered him and his second wife. Elisabeth is now in a California prison and their children are parentless.

Your approach during separation is to keep calm and controlled and maintain a low profile until the divorce is over. If you don't do anything you wouldn't want reported on the front page of your hometown newspaper the next morning, you'll probably be okay.

CHAPTER TEN

Discovery: What It Is and How It Works

IN THIS CHAPTER YOU WILL LEARN:

I. What "discovery" is and why it matters to you
II. The discovery process and five steps for answering questions
III. A checklist to prepare you for discovery
IV. A rehearsal list of questions you may be asked

I. WHAT IS "DISCOVERY" AND WHY DOES IT MATTER TO YOU?

Discovery is the legal name given to the process by which both sides find out everything they can about the other side's case and about the assets and liabilities of the family. In our legal system discovery is encouraged, as is the assumption that justice works better if everything is on the table and everybody on both sides as well as the judge can see what are the true facts and evaluate the fairness of the situation.

Naturally, in an adversarial situation such as a divorce trial, people are often less than enthusiastic about laying all the cards on the table or about what the complete truth is or about that vague concept, "justice." They just want to win. Period. So it is natural that one or the other or both sides will want to keep information to themselves that might help the other side. This is where the discovery process comes into play.

II. THE DISCOVERY PROCESS AND FIVE STEPS FOR ANSWERING QUESTIONS

A. Informal Discovery

As your divorce case begins, there is a stream of informal and voluntary information or discovery coming to your attorney. This comes, initially, from you and from others friendly to you. It will also come from your husband and his attorney as the two opposing attorneys exchange basic information about the case. In the case of an uncontested divorce, much of the information about marital finances and other relevant matters may be gathered in this way. This is fine if you believe that your husband is not going to try to hide assets from you.

B. Formal Discovery

It is more typical that after the informal gathering of information, you and your attorney have to require that information be provided that relates to the finances of the marriage and valuation of assets. These discovery methods can be employed by both you and your husband, and since they are frequently done under the direction of the judge and the court, they attain the status of formal testimony. This is important, because if anyone lies or hides information in formal discovery to distort the outcome of the case and cheat the other, that can be used to appeal rulings that may not be favorable to you. Further, if this underhandedness is discovered before trial, you can use it to undermine your husband's credibility totally.

Formal discovery takes several forms.

1. *Subpoena duces tecum and notice to produce.* You and your attorney can subpoena records and materials needed for your case. A subpoena is an order of the court that is issued to your husband, his employer, his accountant, his colleagues, and his stockbroker to produce relevant documentary material. This is an extremely valuable discovery tool in that it will give your attorney documentary evidence of what the assets and liabilities are and what the operative financial level of the parties has been during marriage.

In some jurisdictions a notice to produce documents is a substitute for a subpoena when used to obtain documents and things from the other party.

2. *Interrogatories.* This discovery method involves the service of a list of questions that you and your attorney want the other side to answer. The recipient of interrogatories is under an obligation by statute to fully answer all the questions, and to the extent necessary, he may be required to search records under his control and obtain information from others over whom that party has some control, such as his accountant or his employer. This procedure may take the place of in-person testimony in a deposition or it may be used in conjunction with a deposition. This discovery device, interrogatories, in some states and in the federal court, can only be used to obtain information from the other party, not third parties. In some states form interrogatories have been developed.

3. *Depositions.* This is testimony given in an informal setting outside the courthouse prior to the trial. A deposition is usually taken at one of the attorney's offices, with a court reporter recording the questions and answers. Again, as a discovery device, the goal is to gather information that may be used to work toward settlement or for trial. If there is an inconsistency between testimony given during a deposition and later testimony by the same witness in court, the witness may be impeached at trial by his or her inconsistent prior testimony. Beyond that, a lie in the deposition is perjury with its attendant criminal penalties. A deposition is just as serious as testifying in court in front of the judge.

Often the person being deposed is required to produce records at depositions such as canceled checks, passbooks, insurance polices, and other financial records of the marriage. In some states, if you don't produce requested records at the deposition, you may not be allowed to produce them at the trial to support your side of the case.

In some sense, a deposition is like testifying in court. It can be intimidating and confusing if you are being deposed, since you probably have never gone through cross examination, which is what it is. You may be intimidated by the presence of your husband at your deposition (and he will be present); you normally can't have friends or relatives along unless they are, in some fashion, involved in the divorce case.

Your attorney will carefully prepare you for your deposition. This preparation will be in the form of at least an hour or two of rehearsal. You will learn the five-step process of responding to questions at a deposition, which is:

1. Listen to the question.
2. Be sure you understand the question.
   If you do not understand the question, say so and ask that the question be rephrased. If the other attorney asks you what part you don't understand, simply say that you do not understand the entire question.
3. Ask yourself if you know the answer.
   Assuming you understand the question, next ask yourself if you know the answer to the question. If you do not, simply say that you don't know the answer to the question.
4. Formulate an answer.
   Assuming you know the answer, the next step is to formulate in your own mind the answer to the question; that means you must decide the words you will use to answer the question.
5. Answer the question.

When you have gone through the four steps set forth above, you are ready to answer the question and only the question asked.

This may seem like a long and complicated exercise. It is not, and it is essential to your giving a good deposition. Not only does this routine give your attorney a chance to object should she wish to, but your answer will be well thought out and will not give the examiner any more information or leads than are necessary.

There are very few questions you may be asked at a deposition that your attorney can legitimately instruct you not to answer. Those that are fall into the category of privileged communications between your lawyer and yourself and any other with whom you have a special relationship, such as your physician, unless that privilege has been waived because you have raised your physical condition as part of the case. This might occur if you contend you are unable to work because of a physical condition that precludes gainful employment.

Your attorney may object to questions that are inartfully formed as being unintelligible, compound, ambiguous, or otherwise confusing. These objections are made to preserve them for trial, but you will still have to answer the question at the deposition. It is important to preserve these objections because an inartfully formed question may be deliberately so. The interrogator may be asking the questions in such a way that, in order to answer it, you have to agree to his assumptions, which may not be true at all. Listen carefully to your lawyer's objections for clues as to what your lawyer is concerned with in the question.

A deposition is not an endurance match, and you may take recesses as needed. Some lawyers will try to take a break between the asking of a difficult question of their client and the answer. This tactic is generally not tolerated by judges in most jurisdictions. You should limit your conversations with your attorney to the essential matters. But, do not hesitate to ask for a recess if you need one for whatever reason.

SPECIAL ASPECTS OF THE DEPOSITION

The deposition is a dress rehearsal for the trial and helps you and your attorney prepare for court. In some ways it may be more difficult than testifying in court, because there are just the two warring sides present without the calming influence of a judge. Beyond that, this may be the first time husband and wife have faced each other since the separation, and the anger and bitterness have had time to germinate and grow. Even so, the deposition serves a valuable tactical purpose having nothing to do with the questions, answers, lies, and bile it produces. It gives your attorney the opportunity to evaluate you, your husband, and other witnesses to see what kind of witnesses the people will be, who is helpful to your case and who isn't. It can help you prepare for testifying in court. It is probably the most expensive type of discovery.

4. *Other formal discovery techniques.* There are several other types of discovery devices authorized by statute that you may be subject to or which your attorney may use. Requests for admissions of fact and to admit the genuineness of documents are designed to commit the responding party to certain facts and to provide foundation for documents that might otherwise not be proper as evidence.

If there is an issue of spousal support, the party seeking support may be subject to an examination by a vocational counselor to determine what employment he can engage in and where. Or, if you lack enough training or experience to support yourself and are what is called a displaced homemaker, your attorney might want to establish that as a basis for long-term spousal support.

For example, today in America some 2.3 million women over the age of thirty-five are experiencing difficulty finding well-paying jobs because they have little or no job experience outside the home. These women are entering the job market because of financial need. Of this group, 42 percent are divorced or separated, 39 percent are married to husbands who are unemployed or disabled, and 19 percent are widows. About half of these people earn less than $10,000 annually, and 75 percent of displaced homemakers earn less than $20,000 per year. In addition, if there is a custody issue both parties may be subject to one or more psychological examinations.

5. *Investigations.* In addition to these methods of discovery, you and your attorney may want to hire private detectives or experts to provide information that will bolster your side of the case. For example, you may want an appraiser to determine the fair market value of certain assets that your husband has depreciated on the family business books so they appear to be of lower value than they would be on the market. It is quite common to have experts determine the value of business and real estate held by the parties.

Or you may want a private investigator to perform what Joe Mullen, one of New York's best detectives, calls an asset search, to locate valuables your husband has stashed away from you. Your husband may be attempting to depress his income temporarily until the divorce is settled by deferring income, bonuses, commissions, and the like until later, for example. If he is in business for himself, this may be easy to do. He might even be taking a vacation or slacking off so that his income will deliberately, but temporarily, drop. If he has stripped the joint bank and investment accounts of money and salted funds away in a secret bank account in his name alone, you will need an investigator to find them. The fact that your husband has placed joint funds in a secret or foreign account doesn't change the fact that it is joint money. The law in some states assumes the spouse taking the funds is holding it in trust for the joint interest. However, you have to find it and prove it exists, and that's where the investigatory part of discovery is important for you and your attorney.

III. A CHECKLIST THAT WILL PREPARE YOU TO FACE "DISCOVERY"

A. The Basic Three Goals of the Opposition

There are hundreds of ways of asking questions about the same subject, and it is not possible for us to crawl inside the head of the opposing attorney to know exactly what questions you will be asked. However, we do know where the opposing attorney is headed, even if we don't know how she plans to get there.

Here are the goals the opposing attorney generally has in mind when she puts you through a deposition, interrogatories, or other discovery process or trial.

1. *Undermine your legal grounds.* If you live in a state where grounds are required for divorce, the opposing attorney may attack your legal grounds for filing for a divorce, which, if successful, ends the case stone-cold dead right there. If you are making claims for separate property, your spouse's attorney will attempt to show that you commingled your property with marital property or that your $25,000 bond was not a gift or a family inheritance at all.

2. *Make you look bad.* Your husband's attorney wants everybody, but the court in particular, to see you in an unsympathetic light, not worthy of alimony, child custody and support, or much of anything else short of a sneer. This is true even in states that have no-fault divorce laws. This type of behavior is generally the normal method of operation of the attorney involved. In other words, she treats everyone like that. In most areas such behavior is frowned upon by other lawyers and not tolerated by the court.

3. *Make your husband look good.* The attorney for your estranged husband wants to paint him as a combination of Prince Charming,

Dr. Spock, and Robin Hood, but principally as the long-suffering supporting spouse who works long hours and gets nothing but bills from Saks in return.

B. Types of Discovery and How to Prepare for Them

1. *Legal.* You may have to prove that you are legally married to your estranged husband. If there is no legal marriage, there cannot be a legal divorce. So be ready to produce a marriage certificate. You may have to be ready to prove that yours was not a bigamous marriage and that it was, to use that delicate euphemism, "consummated," which means in plain English that the two of you had sex. You may have to produce your decree of divorce showing you were actually legally divorced from your prior spouse.

2. *Financial (including property).* You need to be able to identify the marital property that is to be divided. You husband will claim there is nothing beyond the furniture and the cocker spaniel, while you will claim that the marriage owns half of Canada, the English crown jewels, and a time-share condo in Pismo Beach. The truth, of course, lies somewhere in between, but you have to prove what it is with records, witnesses, and testimony. The rule is that you can only split what exists in reality, not just in your imagination.

3. *Lifestyle and conduct.* The fate of minor children is an extremely significant part of the divorce process. Usually one or both of you will seek custody of the children, and this part of discovery is to show which of you is the more competent and better able to share the responsibilities of custody. In theory, the objective is to do what is best for the children by showing who was the principal caregiver of the two of you while you were together, and to establish a schedule and living situation that allows the children to enjoy life with both parents.

4. *Psychological.* Sometimes the issues of money and custody become tangled in your own or your husband's psychological condition or that of your children. Are you and your husband psychologically fit to be custodial parents, or would you actually be unable to provide care or, perhaps, even be a danger to the minor children? A history of alcoholism, drug addiction, sexual and physical abuse, suicide attempts, arrests for threatening, or odd behavior can all shift

the judge's decisions on custody and even money questions. There have been some cases where neither parent has been deemed psychologically competent to have custody of the children, and they are given to grandparents or other relations or foster homes to raise.

IV. A REHEARSAL LIST OF QUESTIONS YOU MAY BE ASKED

Here is a list of the types of questions you might be asked at a normal deposition in which the opposing attorney is trying to obtain information helpful to his client's case in the area of finances and custody. Remember that the opposing attorney wants to make you look bad and his client look good, and the reverse is true when your attorney questions your husband. The trick in answering many of these questions is to give away as little as possible that might hurt your side, yet to answer truthfully and completely each question asked.

To give you a sample of the kind of questions in this short space, we have phrased these in the form of complex questions. Actually, each of the complex questions listed below could well be broken down into four or five questions, each to get at the same point, but you'll get the idea.

And, of course, the opposing counsel may ask questions that you are under no obligation to answer or that should be rephrased for clarity. You should, as we noted earlier, give your attorney a chance to object to each question before you answer it.

- Did you own any real estate in your own name when you got married? Do you still own that real estate and in whose name is it recorded? Improvements to that real estate? Payments on the mortgage? Source of funds for improvements, property taxes, or mortgage payments?
- Did you own any significant personal property such as fine art, antiques, expensive household goods, jewelry, collections, valuable metals, and the like when you married? Where is that now? In whose name is it held?
- Is any of your property or valuables held for you by another person or under a name besides your own? What is it and where is it?

- How many bank accounts do you have in your name alone or shared with someone else? In what bank and at what location are they? What was the balance in each account as of the date of your separation? (Don't guess. Answer by saying you will have to refer to the bank statements.)
- Do you have investments in stocks, bonds, other securities, or other things of exceptional value such as fine art, coins, stamps, collectibles, antiques, rare books, and so one? What are they? When were they acquired? What are they worth in today's market? Where are they?
- Do you have, in your own name or with someone else, a safe-deposit box, storage locker, or other place where you keep important papers and valuable items? Where is it? When was the last time you visited that safe-deposit box or storage locker and why? What are the contents of the safe-deposit box or storage locker?
- Do you anticipate receiving any significant gifts or inheritances in the next two years?
- Has any part of your income from salary, commissions, bonuses, options, or other sources changed significantly in the last three years? How much and why? Do you anticipate any significant changes in the next three years? How much and why? What is your ability to work? What are your work-related degrees or licenses? What are your work skills? What is your work experience?
- Who usually sees that the children get to and from school and who deals with the school authorities and teachers most of the time?
- Who takes care of the children's day-to-day needs such as dressing them, washing their clothes, driving them to and from school and other activities, helping them with their homework, and routinely disciplining them?
- Have you ever sexually abused one of your children by inappropriate touching, kissing, caressing, inserting, fondling, hurting, beating, or forcing your sexual attentions on that child?
- Have you ever sought therapy or been under the care of a psychologist, psychiatrist, psychological counselor, or

ordained religious professional for unusual, odd, or abnormal behavior?
- Have you ever been arrested, convicted of a felony, served time in prison? What was the charge, circumstances, and outcome of this encounter with the law?
- Do you use or abuse alcohol, prescription drugs, illegal substances now or have you ever done so?
- Have you ever had a sexually transmitted disease?
- Have you ever lied in making out an application for a loan or credit card? Or on your income tax return? (Without foundation, these questions are improper and should be objected to by your lawyer.) Have you ever been turned down for credit or a loan or a charge account or a credit card? When, by whom, and why?
- Have you ever struck, locked up and confined, or physically disciplined any of your children? Describe the circumstances and what happened in detail.
- Have you had sexual relations during your marriage with anyone other than your spouse? During your marriage, have you ever engaged in perverse, unusual, or exotic sexual practices with anyone other than your spouse? Describe the circumstances.
- Do you have a preference as to what property is awarded to you?
- Describe what you do for a living and give us a brief employment history since you left school. Are you now employed? If so, where, in what capacity, for how long, and what compensation have you received in total, including deferred income, pensions, vestings, and bonuses to be paid in the future?

The deposition could take a few hours or even a few days, and the opposing attorney will peek, poke, and pry into every aspect of you, your history, your life, and your competence. These sample questions will give you some idea of what to expect. It usually is not pretty, but it has to be endured. And remember, your husband will have to go through it, too.

THE BIG SECRET TO DOING WELL IN A DEPOSITION

It's simple: Rehearse beforehand. Have your attorney or someone from her office put you through several hours of a mock deposition. They should be as mean as junkyard dogs and grill you on everything, trying to make you lose your temper, tell a lie, get crossed up, and be totally miserable. If they are tough enough on you in the private rehearsal for the deposition, then the actual deposition will go much more smoothly and be easier for you.

FOUR POINTERS ON DOING WELL DURING THE DEPOSITION

1. Follow the five steps for response to deposition questions that are set forth earlier in this chapter.
2. Rehearse.
3. Dress neatly and conservatively.
4. Be polite and serious. Keep your cool.

CHAPTER ELEVEN

Getting Ready for Trial

IN THIS CHAPTER YOU WILL LEARN:

I. How to prepare for your court appearance and trial
II. What you need to know before showing up in court
III. What to expect during the trial
IV. Some unpleasant truths about being in court
V. Words you should know to understand what's going on

I. HOW TO PREPARE FOR YOUR COURT APPEARANCE AND TRIAL

Despite the fact that most divorce proceedings settle before trial, there are some that do not or that settle on the courthouse steps on the very day of trial. Either way, you must be prepared for the possibility that your fate will be decided by a black-robed third party and *you* will have the responsibility of helping that judge see things your way.

A. The Easy Way

If all has gone smoothly, you and your husband will approach your appearance in court with most things settled. In days gone by, that normally meant you got the house, the children, some bank or investment accounts, and your car. Your husband got the business or career assets, some bank or investment accounts, and his car and personal property, along with the obligation of paying alimony and child support.

In today's topsy-turvy world of life and divorce, that scenario could drastically change: Your husband might have custody of the kids; you may be the major wage earner, and he may be the spouse receiving the alimony. Still, as we said, all of this might be settled in the pretrial settlement conference and negotiations, resulting in a settlement agreement without trial.

B. The Hard Way

However, it is not always possible to resolve everything through the settlement process. Some issues may have to be decided by the judge when she puts her stamp of approval on the pretrial agreement that disposes of most other disputes. Trial by a judge is time-consuming and more expensive than settlement, but it often cannot be avoided.

THE QUIRKY TRUTH ABOUT UNSETTLED ISSUES IN DIVORCE

It is a strange truth about us human beings and about settlement negotiations that very often the unresolved issue between people turns out to be what outsiders regard as a trivial matter. For husband and wife it is a sentimental item or a matter of principle, and when "a matter of principle" walks in the door, common sense flies out the window. Husbands and wives have been prepared to divide hundreds of thousands of dollars' worth of property with the snap of a finger and then arm-wrestle to the death over a plastic Buddha figurine or a pet armadillo.

C. Pretrial Preparation

There are three levels of preparation you need to undertake and accomplish before going to the courtroom for the trial. You may feel that the facts of your case are so obvious and so strong in your favor that the issues will be resolved simply and quickly in your favor and that's it. The truth is that the facts are important, but there other factors that can affect the outcome of your case, and these are what you must be prepared to deal with before the trial.

1. *Mental preparation.* You must have a clear understanding of the issues and procedures that will occur at the trial. There should be no surprises that will catch you off guard. Ideally, your attorney should walk you through each step of the trial and, in essence, do a dry run of the trial with you. All of this costs attorney time and money.

You must have a solid understanding of the points to be made to prove your side of the case. Write these down and go over them several times, until they are etched in your memory as if you are boning up for a test in school, because the outcome of this test will determine the next few years of your life.

Have your attorney review with you what she anticipates will be the responses of your spouse.

What will his arguments be and what is your rebuttal? Understand this process and keep the facts in mind. If you do, you will be prepared to answer most of the other side's arguments and quite capable of understanding the process of the trial.

Your lawyer should carefully brief you on how to testify. She should go over the questions you will probably be asked, as well as how you should answer.

Your attorney should brief you on how you should dress and behave in court and tell you what you need to bring with you to the trial. In most instances, your attorney will have prepared the documentary evidence called exhibits. However, there may be records discovered at the last minute that you need to bring with you. Unless you anticipate testimony requiring a calculation, you should be prepared to testify without notes. Anything that you refer to during your testimony is open to inspection and questioning by your husband's attorney, and your testimony may be suspect if you must refer to notes in order to testify to facts that occurred in your life.

At this pretrial briefing with your attorney you will discuss with her your concerns about the trial. What are the things you are afraid of or apprehensive about? Again, make a list.

Finally, both you and your attorney should try to psych out the other side's "surprises." In other words, candidly consider all the worst things that might happen at the trial, the worst witnesses who may appear, and the worst evidence that could be presented at the trial, no matter how unlikely it is that one of these surprises will surface at the trial. Are there any dark, shameful secrets that you have that could be produced to embarrass you and weaken your case? Financial or sexual or criminal scandals? Your secret diary? A so-called "best friend" who suddenly shows up to testify for the other side? Always go into the courtroom prepared to deal with the worst that the other side can offer.

2. *Psychological preparation.* We will not minimize the stress of a divorce trial—it is not a pleasant experience to try in the public court, before a stranger, the difficult, unresolved issues of your marriage. It probably falls somewhere between the tension of a wedding and root canal work on the scale of stressful events in your life. It may, for example, be the first time you have seen your husband in some time, and you may be filled with anger, hatred, and vengeance, all of which are things you *must* leave at home that day.

The judge or jury who will decide the outcome of your divorce are strongly affected by the personal appearance and behavior of the two parties in court. So, you must be on your best behavior—reasonable, sensitive, and above all honest. You could hurt your case with a bad attitude or offensive behavior, even if the law is on your side.

We strongly urge that you be cautious of your possible proclivity to nag or appear to be a battle-ax who hectors and harasses her husband. Remember, the judge or some members of the jury may also be such husbands. The psychological image you want to convey in that courtroom is that of a sympathetic, perhaps spurned spouse, a good mother, supportive of your ex in his business endeavors, but, please, not a victim. Present yourself as a reasonable and dignified person, sad that what was once a happy marriage has finally come to an end—no arrogance and no hostility.

3. *Physical preparation.* Your physical appearance conveys a strong message to the court, and you should be careful about what you wear, how your hair is done, how you are made up, and the total

image you project. Dress conservatively. No flashy hairdo or makeup, no spike heels, no miniskirts or plunging necklines, no loud colors. You should look like a schoolmarm or preacher's wife. Even if you find it distasteful that you have to play such a role, do it. The courtroom is not the place for some kind of social or fashion statement. You are trying to win a court case, and if you present the wrong image to the judge, your husband may not win so much as you may lose.

TRIAL PREPARATION TIP

Sometime before the trial select your clothes—dress, shoes, hose, accessories—and have everything ready for that day. Have money for transportation, parking, etc., and any passes or checks you need handy, and the court address, phone, and room number written down, along with the name of the judge. Then put it all aside in plastic bags in the closet so everything is set for that day and you don't have to rush around at the last minute getting something dry cleaned or buying something at the store. This will help ease the pressure on you the day of the trial. Arrange for a friend or relative to take the children to school that day.

II. WHAT YOU NEED TO KNOW BEFORE YOUR COURT APPEARANCE

A. The Burden of Proof Is on You

1. *Witnesses.* Witnesses are an important part of the trial. These people will help to establish the extent and value of the marital property. Their testimony will form the basis of the fair division between you and your soon-to-be ex-husband. If there is a custody battle, each parent will produce witnesses to attest to their capabilities as parents. Teachers, close friends, other parents will be called to testify about the relationship between you and the children, to establish that you are a sensitive, reliable, and competent mother—in short, a

good mom whose children's interests will be best served by primary custody being with you. These witnesses can also establish that the father is distant, distracted, and rarely around to take care of the kids when he is needed, that he is away from home often and that he hadn't been involved in the children's school, medical care, hygiene, and discipline. In short, you are looking for witnesses to establish that your husband is, generally, an absentee father with neither the time nor the interest to be a good dad. This line of defense in a custody battle may impress you and possibly the judge. But remember, usually one parent has to work. Don't overdo the absentee father theory because it is quite possible that Dad's absence is explained by the necessity to support his family, including your extraordinary spending habits. Now that you will be on a budget imposed by court-ordered support, he may not have to work such long hours and may be able to spend more time with the child.

Witnesses should not just be called in any willy-nilly order. There is a science and an art to the presentation of a successful case. It is much like the development of theme, motive, character, and plot in a play, where the sequence of characters and what they reveal at what time is critical to making the strongest play (case), both factually and emotionally.

Suppose, for example, the strategy that you and your attorney have worked out goes something like this: You were unable before the trial to obtain your husband's agreement to all the issues in the settlement conferences, but you think that, if you can force him back to the settlement conference table, you can now get him to give on important points. So what you may want to do, now that you are both forced to go to trial, is to convince your husband that it would be easier, cheaper, and less embarrassing for him to return to the settlement conference and work out your differences in private.

To achieve the reinstitution of settlement discussion, you and your attorney may decide to put on your strongest and most damaging witnesses at the very beginning of the trial to convince your husband that this is not a case he wants tried in a public courtroom, nor is it a case he can win. Having done that, your attorney might privately suggest to your husband's attorney that we all go back to the settlement conference for one more try at a private resolution of the differences between you. If the other side agrees, the two attorneys may then interrupt the trial and suggest to the judge that there be a day or two recess because the parties think they might be able to settle their problems privately. Most judges will welcome such relief to the court calendar and will grant some arrangement that allows resumption of the settlement discussions. In fact, many judges will ask the lawyers from time to time during the trial if it isn't possible to reach an agreement between the husband and wife without continuing the trial.

Witnesses called by either side may be tricky or create unexpected, and certainly unwanted, problems. A witness for you who is easily confused or intimidated by the other attorney can hurt you more than help you. You and your attorney have to assess beforehand who are the witnesses who will do well for you. You may decide to eliminate all others from your witness list. Do not, for example, call a witness just because that witness is a friend of yours and would be insulted if you didn't let him or her speak out on your behalf. This is not a school play where everybody in the class gets a part. This is a real-life drama, and whether or not you get a fair deal on the property and custody of the children depends on the presentation given by you and your witnesses.

Each side will call experts skilled in the valuation of real estate, fine art or securities, business or partnership appraisal. Child psychologists, physicians, and perhaps psychiatrists may be called as witnesses. Just be sure, if the other side is calling in experts, that you have your own experts to refute the first experts' testimony. Of course, the lawyers for each side will try to destroy the credibility of the other side's expert witnesses. (This procedure should cause you to weigh carefully the advantages of hiring joint experts with the reserved right to hire your own if the expert is truly off base and to resolve, with the assistance of your individual attorneys, these issues yourselves.)

Some troublesome witnesses may include relatives, close family or friends, the children, and even *you*. Be prepared for this by reviewing with your attorney what each witness's probable testimony will be, both good and bad. Alert your attorney to any situation in the lives of these potential adverse witnesses that might be used to cast doubt on their credibility, such as criminal convictions, mental illness, longstanding hatred and desire for revenge, or prejudice, or facts indicating bias.

It is essential to prepare your witnesses before the trial by putting them through a dry run in your attorney's office, asking them both the questions your attorney will ask and the questions the opposing attorney will probably ask.

Hostile witnesses, as we mention elsewhere, are not friendly to your side, but can serve a useful purpose. Sometimes they can reveal important information you can't get from another source because even hostile witnesses are reluctant to lie on the witness stand for fear of being punished for perjury. If such a witness projects a bad image and he or she is clearly hostile to you, that can make you look good.

2. *Exhibits.* It is not universally true, but in most cases judges love documents, reports, and other written "proof," especially if it comes from "official" sources or reliable experts. Thus, reports from credible Certified Public Accountants, appraisers, government assessors, tax departments, schools, institutions, police departments, court case records, and even your own bank records will carry significant weight with the judge. This is because, theoretically, documents do not lie (unless altered), but people do.

No one likes to appear uninformed or stupid, and that is particularly true with people in such prestigious positions as judges. Still, no one understands everything about finances or complex transactions. In an appropriate case your attorney will prepare charts and graphs to display in picture form the testimony of a witness. This document is different from documents created outside the divorce context, such as tax returns or deeds.

There is, of course, a growing body of records that take the form of audio- and videotapes and films. Some courts permit introduction of these electronically recorded documents into evidence and others do not. Generally, admissibility of such a "document" is dependent upon your attorney establishing a foundation for the document. And, of course, there may be questionable materials that your husband may seek to introduce. Whether or not such documents will be allowed in evidence is up to the trial judge. Clients are often concerned about material and records one spouse has stolen from the other or photos and tapes made secretly by one spouse that may embarrass or incriminate the other spouse. If these materials are relevant to the subject matter of the lawsuit and legally obtained, they may be admitted into evidence.

B. The Arbitration Card

Court dockets are jammed and judges overworked. Because of this you may have a sympathetic ear when you propose a procedure that will ease her workload: Try binding arbitration. What this means is you remove the issue from the public court and take it to a private judge, who will make a decision that is binding on you.

Unless the judge orders a case to a referee for a recommendation that he or she will adopt, the only way you can move your case to binding arbitration is by agreement of the parties. You may suggest a private judge to the other side whom you are willing to accept to settle the matter through such arbitration.

The judge in the public court can rule on the status of the divorce—that is, whether you continue to be husband and wife—and include a finding that reserves jurisdiction over all other issues. Some you and your husband may settle; others you will take to a private judge for binding arbitration. This means that a neutral arbitrator or arbitrators are selected and you each present your case to the arbitrator(s), who then make a judgment, and both you and your husband are bound by that judgment. Professional arbitrators are available from various sources, with the most popular one being the American Arbitration Association (AAA) at 140 West 51st Street, New York, NY 10020. The AAA is listed in the phone books of most major cities. In most states there is an ever-increasing supply of judges retired from the public court system who welcome these cases.

III. WHAT TO EXPECT DURING THE TRIAL

A. Trial Procedure

There is a certain procedure for the conduct of a trial and presentation of the evidence. In most instances the judge will insist that the attorneys follow this procedure, although some variation may be had for the convenience of out-of-town or expert witnesses. Sometimes, in family law cases, a judge will allow, or even demand, that the respondent present most of his case at the same time as he is cross-examining the petitioner's witnesses, in that the same witnesses he would have called are called in the petitioner's case. This is a judicially acceptable method of shortening the trial. However, it puts the respondent at a disadvantage in that the orderly presentation of his case is disrupted. If your attorney has a choice, she should demand that the case be presented in the following order:

1. *Pretrial conference.* Before the trial begins, there should be agreement on what the issues are—what is the objective everyone is trying to achieve and what are the outstanding factual and legal disagreements. Generally the lawyers for each side and the judge will meet before formally starting the trial to set out the issues and the procedure to be followed. These are the possibilities:

　　a. **All issues are settled.** If all issues are settled at the pretrial settlement conference and an agreement between husband and wife is signed or put on the record, there is no need for a trial, and you can skip steps 2 through 5 and move on to the judicial decision approving your agreement. In that case the judge will review the settlement agreement to determine if it is in compliance with the law and is in proper form, with appropriate protections for the children. That's it. It's over.

　　b. **All issues are not settled.** If there are any outstanding issues—even if most issues were settled—there will be a trial to reach a determination of the unresolved issues. The remaining issues will be agreed upon by the attorneys for both sides after the pretrial conference. Fortunately for the overloaded court system and the sanity of most people involved, the number of cases that go to trial are relatively few—probably less than 5 percent of the divorces filed.

2. *Opening statements.* This is the formal beginning of the trial. Each lawyer presents to the court what it is that they expect to prove about each of the unresolved issues. The opening statement may even be much like what we've all seen on *Perry Mason* and *Law and Order.* It will follow the ancient pattern of teaching or speech making: you begin by telling the audience what you're going to tell them; then you tell them; and finally you tell them what you've told them. So the opening statement is telling the judge or jury what you're going to prove for them.

3. *Petitioner's case.*

　　a. **Direct examination.** The attorney for the petitioner (you in our scenario) calls you and your other witnesses, which may include your husband, and presents your documentary evidence.

b. **Cross-examination.** After each witness is examined on direct by the petitioner's counsel, the lawyer for your husband, the respondent, is allowed to ask questions on cross-examination, which must be within the framework or the scope of the direct examination. If she strays from that, your attorney may object to the question as being outside the scope of direct. The court may or may not allow the question, depending on how closely the judge wants to stay within recognized trial procedures. Sometimes the judge will suggest that the cross-examiner take the witness as a hostile witness, giving the opportunity for a broadened scope of questioning. The ideal is to limit cross-examination to the scope of the direct examination.

c. **Redirect examination.** After cross-examination, your attorney may ask the same witness questions on redirect in an attempt to rehabilitate the witness from any undermining of the witness's testimony as a result of the cross-examination.

d. **Recross-examination.** The respondent's attorney also has an opportunity for further examination for the purpose of undermining the direct testimony.

This procedure is followed for each witness until the petitioner has completed the examination of all her witnesses. The judge will ask if the petitioner rests. If she does, then it is the respondent's turn to present his case.

4. *Respondent's case.* The presentation of the evidence is handled in much the same way for the respondent's case through direct, cross, redirect, and recross-examination.

5. *Closing arguments.* After the conclusion of the presentation of all evidence, both through live testimony and documentary evidence, and both sides have rested, the court will generally allow time for the attorneys to argue the evidence in an attempt to convince the judge that their side's version of the facts is right. Often, particularly in the case of a long trial, the judge will ask for written argument. So the attorneys will go back to their offices and put together a review of the evidence, citing testimony and documentary evidence again, in an effort to bring the court around to their view of the facts and the applicability of the law to the facts.

6. *Court's decision.* After all the evidence and argument has been presented by both sides, you then come to the only words that count: the judge's words. At this point all the unresolved issues are put in

the judge's hands for a final decision. Sometimes, depending on the length of the trial and complexity of the issues, the judge will pronounce his decision from the bench at this point in the trial, or he or she may take all that has been presented by each side "under advisement" or "under submission," which means the judge wants to think about the case and will render a decision at a later time. In any case, the trial is over for you and your husband, and all that remains at this stage is the judge's decision.

IV. SOME UNPLEASANT TRUTHS ABOUT BEING IN COURT

A. Your Dirty Linen Will Be Publicized

Naturally, one of the aspects of court you will not like is the washing of the family dirty linen in public. That's usually embarrassing for us because we don't want the world to know about our weaknesses, peccadilloes, sexual habits, morality, and personal hygiene, all of which may be presented by the other side to prove you are an unworthy wife, mother, woman, and member of the human race and the court would be doing the world a favor to send you to pasture. Your attorney, of course, will be playing the same game with your husband's reputation and sensibilities. A public court trial is exactly that, public.

On the other hand, you should not take this too seriously, because unless you or your husband are celebrities, the chances are that nobody outside of the courtroom will ever hear about what was said or went on at the trial. You will find sitting in the courtroom on the day of your hearing two categories of people: first, those who also have a trial pending and are probably consumed with their own troubles and not paying much attention to your problems; second, the judge and court personnel, who have heard all of this kind of slanderous dirt a zillion times before and frankly are no longer shocked, titillated, or interested.

B. There May Be Surprise Witnesses and Evidence

One of the bitter truths found in many divorce trials is the sudden appearance of surprise witnesses and evidence. You may be stunned when somebody whom you thought was your best friend or one of your children or a member of your family shows up in the courtroom as *a witness for the other side!* Or that the confidential diary that you thought was secretly hidden away, or the secret bank account or safe-deposit box that you thought nobody knew about, surprisingly appears as part of the exhibits presented by the other side.

C. You May Be a Witness for Your Husband

Many wives are aghast to discover that they can be called to the stand in the courtroom as a witness by their husband's attorney. Obviously, you would be a hostile witness, but as we said before that doesn't mean you will not be called in your husband's case for the purpose of proving one of his contentions. The objective may be to obtain information by forcing you to tell something you have been concealing. Or the objective frequently may not be to obtain information but to make you look bad by casting doubt on your honesty, or by inciting you to lose your temper and attack your husband verbally, or generally to come across as an unpleasant, unreasonable person. So the facts may not hurt you as much as your own image.

D. You Will Be the Target of Your Husband's Attorney

Understand that the job of your husband's attorney is to paint you as a nagging, money-spending, lazy woman, a bad mother, and not the loving, caring, competent wife you really are. He will try to portray you as an evil person. He will try to embarrass you, trap you into contradictions and misstatements, and cause you to lose your cool. That will hurt your case, and you have to control yourself so it doesn't happen. You must maintain your composure and simply answer the questions asked. Your attorney will object if the other attorney becomes overzealous.

E. At Times You Will Be on Your Own

The stark reality you must understand and prepare for in your own mind is that your lawyer can't save you all the time. This is a corollary of the immediately preceding point. There will be times during the trial when you will be entirely on your own, without help from your attorney. For example, suppose your husband's attorney asks you a question you feel is tough, mean, embarrassing, hostile, cruel. Your attorney will probably be on her feet in a flash and object to the question, demanding that it be withdrawn. However, if the judge overrules your attorney and directs you to answer the question, that is what you have to do. At that point you are on your own, and you have to handle the situation on your own. This is why we continually make the point throughout this book that you *must* be involved in your case, know all the details, and be prepared to handle any part of it on your own without help. If you do this, you will not be helpless when forced to answer questions that embarrass you or when you are put in a tight situation.

F. Hidden Scandals Will Explode in Your Face

Never make the mistake of assuming that some scandal in your life will not be uncovered and used against you. You are wrong. First, your husband probably knows about it and has told his attorney. Or his attorney has had a private detective look into your past and is ready to produce pictures, witnesses, and documents. Or—and this happens more often than you might think—your best friend turns on you and confesses to something the two of you did together or something that she knows you did.

So if you have done time for drugs or prostitution or were a top-less dancer at the local truck stop or you are a fugitive from justice or a bigamist or whatever, clue your attorney in on it and on every other dark secret that can be used to make you look bad in court. If you have or contemplate other relationships with either a man or a woman, it will come out. You must prepare a counteroffensive or, at least, a defense if the issue comes up. Or you may want to reveal the dark secret yourself immediately, explain it away as a youthful indiscretion or a temporary condition that has now been corrected and show that you are fully rehabilitated and present witnesses and documents to prove it. That takes the wind out of any attack by your husband and earns you points for maturity and honesty. And, of course, the explosive revelation might go the other way. In the 1991 divorce case of Hermi and Milan Jedlicka, Hermi accused Milan of having murdered George M. Perry in 1983, and the authorities immediately reopened their investigation of Milan in connection with that killing.

G. Children Can Be the Most Dangerous Witnesses

Most child psychologists will warn you that children are very unreliable as witnesses. We do not really understand all the variables at work inside the child's mind. This is one reason young children usually testify in chambers and then only sparingly about their own feelings as related to custody, visiting rights, and their own safety. There are some basic facts that seem generally understood about children and their court testimony. They realize early on in disputes between their parents not to take sides and that their own survival depends on some adult. They have learned at a young age what makes their adult tick, so they know what buttons to push to be cared for, fed, protected, and sheltered. Secondly, while they don't understand why adults do all the things they do, children are notorious survivors who will do and say whatever is necessary to survive, no matter the turmoil the adults have made of their world. So, if it is necessary to lie or pretend something that isn't true to survive, most children will do it and will believe it.

Obviously, not all children are allowed to testify in court. Usually the judge insists that the child be old enough to understand right and wrong and to understand in simple terms what is happening. Whether a child will be allowed to express his or her views about custody varies with different judges. Some judges feel that they are better equipped to make custody decisions without input from the children, even if the child is as old as thirteen or fourteen or more, ages when most children have very definite ideas about what they want and where they want to be. Bring your children to court only after considerable thought. It will affect them, and their statements to the judge, assuming she will tell you what they are, may surprise you.

V. WORDS YOU SHOULD KNOW TO UNDERSTAND WHAT'S GOING ON

Here again, we want to familiarize you with some of the technical jargon used in the trial that you should understand, so that you will be able to appreciate what is going on in your case as it happens.

In camera. This term means that all or part of the trial is held in private—often in the judge's chambers—because of the sensitive nature of the material, usually involving the children or perhaps trade secrets. There may be testimony that could damage the reputation of one of the people involved if publicly revealed. Judges will often take the testimony of children in chambers or make a sensitive document inspections *in camera*. However, because the First Amendment guarantees the right of access to the courts by the press, if you are concerned about public discussion of your assets or other sensitive issues, consider a private judge.

Hostile witness. This is a witness who is antagonistic to one side of the case. A *hostile witness* is sometimes called because he or she has information not available from any other source. To the surprise of many people, each party to the divorce has the right to call his or her spouse to testify. Such a witness is a hostile witness. Another example is your husband's long-time secretary, who will do anything for him, including commit perjury. The reason for using such witnesses is that experience shows that even hostile witnesses will sometimes tell the truth when under oath on the stand. Certainly, if they do not they are subject to severe penalties for perjury themselves.

Subpoena. This is a court order directing a witness to appear or to produce some kind of documentation (*subpoena duces tecum*). A *subpoena* is used to compel the appearance of witnesses before the court who might not appear voluntarily.

Exhibits. This is physical evidence that each side uses to prove points for its case. In a divorce case the court would expect to be presented with legal or financial documents or reports from experts.

CHAPTER TWELVE

The Trial

IN THIS CHAPTER YOU WILL LEARN MORE
ABOUT THE ACTUAL TRIAL:

I. Going to court
II. Your dress and behavior—*this is important!*
III. The questioning
IV. Typical issues to be settled at a trial
V. How to be a strong witness for your side
VI. Helpful words and phrases
VII. Trial secrets you should know but nobody tells you

I. GOING TO COURT

We talked in the last chapter about many of the things you need to do to prepare for your appearance in court. Here we will expand on parts of that. Read the last chapter and this one carefully, as if you were preparing for a starring role in a stage play, because in many ways that is exactly what you are doing. You are starring in one of the most important public appearances you will ever make because it will determine much of your life and lifestyle for years to come.

You will be a success if you carry yourself with dignity and are courteous to everyone. Those you encounter will admire you for your poise and control in the face of a tough emotional experience. Never appear to be vengeful or mean. Come across as sad that it has all come to this but determined to see it through, doing what is right and fair for yourself and for the children.

TIP TO GET YOU STARTED RIGHT

In the last chapter, we suggested how to avoid the last-minute rush to get ready. Now we suggest how to start out the trial day easier. A few days or a week before your trial date, make a dry run. Go down to the courthouse where your case will be tried. You will find the best route for getting there, what public transportation to take or where to park if you are driving, and how much it will cost. Then, go into the courthouse and find the courtroom so you will have no trouble finding it on the day of your trial. It would be a good idea for you to go into that courtroom or another one nearby and spend a few hours just sitting and watching someone else's divorce trial. This will give you a sense of what goes on and won't make it so strange or intimidating on the day of your trial. This will take a few hours out of your day, but it is well worth it in preparing for one of the most important days of your life.

Be sure you have reviewed with your attorney what you need to bring to the trial. You may need to bring a few things, such as a child's recently received report card or yesterday's angry note from your husband advising you to get rid of your attorney and settle with him. Make sure you and your attorney coordinate so that nothing is left behind and unavailable when needed in the trial just because the two of you did not communicate and double-check with each other.

In many states your attorney will have put together a trial brief that summarizes the statistical details of the marriage, the grounds for the divorce, your contentions, the legal support for your contentions and for the amount you are seeking for support, your proposed division of the property, and your suggestions regarding custody. This makes the judge's work easier and it gives her a better grasp of your particular case.

Your plan for dividing the property will list all the property in the marriage that is joint property, the fair market value, the encumbrances, and all other debts and obligations. Your proposal should set forth your ideas as to how this property should be divided, who gets what, and what future orders for spousal support and child support are appropriate. Obviously, your proposal is just that. It reflects your contentions, and the opposing side will file a conflicting plan. If your plan is reasonable, well thought out, and simple, the judge is highly likely to accept it as a model for decision in the case.

II. YOUR DRESS AND BEHAVIOR— *THIS IS IMPORTANT!*

We've said it before and we'll say it again, because of the importance that your personal appearance and demeanor may have to the decision. Your appearance should be that of a mature, conservative, and traditional woman. Dress in modest and conservative clothes. Keep the makeup and hair toned down and not brassy. Conduct yourself in a restrained manner and be polite to everyone, including your husband and his lawyer, despite how you really feel about them.

Being loud, aggressive, argumentative, and irrational can hurt your case, regardless of what your legal position is.

III. THE QUESTIONING

The trial will proceed generally along the lines we outlined in the previous chapter, with each side having a chance to present its case and to rebut the case of the opposition. You should pay close attention to the proceedings and make notes on the points made by the other witnesses and the exhibits that are introduced. This is to prepare yourself for the last-minute thoughts you may have about your own answers to questions that may arise as a result of the testimony of another witness. Something that is said in the course of the trial may refresh your recollection on the subject, and you will want to communicate your thoughts to your attorney. For example, if another witness reveals something surprising and damaging to you, your attorney and you will caucus in the courtroom to decide what you may say to counter that testimony or to provide ammunition to undermine that witness on cross-examination. If you have prepared as carefully as we urged you to do in the previous chapter, there should be no surprise that you can't handle effectively.

COURT ETIQUETTE POINTER

Do not talk to your attorney while other witnesses are being questioned. She wants to follow the questioning. If you have something to say to your attorney, put it on paper. You should come equipped with a note pad and plenty of pens.

One of the most frustrating things about the trial is that you may not be able to determine at the time the evidence is coming in what effect it is having, because you will not know how the judge is processing it in his mind. The same facts can on occasion lead to different conclusions, and you should understand that. Remember no matter how much you want this divorce and how anxious you are to have your day in court, that day will be an aggravating day for you. Eat well but lightly, and certainly avoid tranquilizers, drugs, or booze. These can incapacitate you on the witness stand. Focus on the end result, namely, you are going to be free and ready for a new and better life tomorrow even if you have to go through this personal hell today.

If it is any comfort, keep in mind that this is a grimly unpleasant day for your husband, too. Your attorney will be trying to take as much of the marital property from him as he can and to convince the judge that he was and is a vile, vicious, and venal man not worthy of you and certainly not a suitable custodial parent for the children. The divorce trial is not a triumph for either side, and if you come out of it with a fair share of the money and a reasonable custodial plan that is in the best interests of the children, you are a winner—or, at least, less of a loser than you might have been.

IV. TYPICAL ISSUES TO BE RESOLVED AT A TRIAL

A. Spousal Support

The three basic questions on this issue are:

1. *Will alimony be paid?* If there is a significant difference between what the spouses earn, or if what the lesser-earning spouse earns is insufficient to support herself, the chances are very good that the principal wage earner will have to pay alimony or spousal support.

Family Law in the Fifty States— Basis for Alimony *

View of Recent Cases in Various States

- ARKANSAS
  In *Busby v. Busby* the court looked beyond the couple's net income to their total earning ability settlement and the ill health of the wife. It ordered the husband to pay $35 a week in alimony, even though the wife already received $1,200 a month in benefits because she had bone cancer, no job, and heavy medical expenses.

- VERMONT
  Downs v. Downs involved a doctor husband and considered the future benefits of his degree, repayment of school loans, and buying into a medical partnership in setting the alimony. An important factor cited was the standard of living each of the spouses had and said the wife was entitled to more than just enough to meet her needs.

- IOWA
  In the Weiss case, the court took into consideration the inherited and gifted property of each of the spouses. Even though that is separate property and not subject to division between the divorcing spouses, the court used the property as a measure of whether or not alimony was appropriate or necessary.

  * *Interpretations of the law vary from state to state and from time to time. These views are only illustrations, and you should check with current rulings in your own state.*

2. *By whom and to whom?* The basic grounds for an award of support are need and ability to pay. Thus, if a spouse can prove a need by demonstrating that the family standard of living is not something she can maintain on her salary if she is working or that she is not working at all and there is a good reason for her not working, she will have proved her need for support. The second and equal issue is ability to pay. The paying spouse must be shown to be capable of paying support to the other spouse. This involves evidence of that spouse's income and sources of income.

3. *How much and how long?* Usually the monthly sum to be paid is an amount consistent with what the principal wage earner makes, the couple's predivorce lifestyle, and the responsibilities of each after the divorce. Some of the factors that courts may take into account are the length of the marriage; the alimony-receiving spouse's ability to earn a living; her age, health, and educational background; and the fact that she did not finish her own education in order to enable her husband to finish his. The judge will consider the contribution of the supported spouse in staying at home to raise the children of the parties and, finally, what is realistic to expect her to earn on her own. The wife's contribution to the marriage that assisted in the accumulation of the marital property is also a factor.

In a marriage that lasted only a few years, there may be no permanent spousal support paid, while for a marriage that lasted from ten to twenty-five years, spousal support will be substantial and long term. The lifestyle of the couple during marriage is also considered. What is fair in the average marriage cannot be compared with a situation like that of convicted multimillionaire stock swindler Ivan Boesky, whose wife had to pay him $20,000 a month, an amount consistent with their married lifestyle, which may have resulted from his illicit gains.

In some jurisdictions the court may impose a cutoff date for payment of alimony in the event that there is a reasonable expectation that the supported spouse's need for support will decrease or terminate. However, in many jurisdictions a court may not terminate the right to receive alimony if the marriage is one of long duration. In California this amounts to ten years. Unless the parties agree to the contrary, alimony is terminated on remarriage of the supported spouse. This, of course, inevitably leads to the alimony-receiving spouse sneaking around living with the new lover, but avoiding marriage because it would cut off the alimony. Thus in some divorce settlements it may be wise to provide an incentive for the supported spouse to marry, such as a lump sum payment if she marries within two years of the divorce. In one case we are aware of, the paying spouse paid for the former wife's wedding.

Divorcing spouses are always looking for some easy way to calculate the amount of support to be paid and the length of time they will be paying it. In some jurisdictions computer programs have been developed to calculate spousal support. The rule of thumb in some jurisdictions is 40 percent of gross income less half of the earnings of the supported spouse. Thus, if a supporting spouse's gross income is $100,000 and the supported spouse's gross income is $20,000, the supported spouse will be entitled to receive $30,000 ($100,000 ¥ .40 = $40,000 less 1/2 of $20,000 = $30,000). How about length of time during which support may be paid? In jurisdictions that allow a termination without a showing of reduced need, the rule of thumb is that support will be paid for half the length of time of the marriage. This is most often applicable to short marriages.

B. Child Custody

Here again, the basic questions are simple, it's just the answers that get complicated. The basic questions include:

> Who shall be the primary custodial parent?
> What visitation or custodial rights does the other parent
> receive?

The testimony to be given in a child custody case focuses on what is in the best interests of the children. You and your husband will try to establish who is the most nurturing of the parents; which, if either, parent has a closer psychological tie with the children; which parent has the time and inclination to provide the best care and environment for the children. In other words, examining all the facts and circumstances regarding the living conditions of the parents and the children, how will the children's best interests be served.

Until recently, it was assumed that mothers were better suited for the custodial care of younger children (this was called "the tender years doctrine"). Presumably this evolved from the fact that mothers were exactly that and the more nurturing of the parents, and since women generally did not work outside the home, they were most often available to care for the children. The result was that it was assumed that the custody of young children, and even those in their teen years, remained with the mother. However, this is not the case in more recent times, with more than half the women in the country holding a full-time job outside the home and sometimes being the sole or principal wage earner in the family. Women live less cloistered lives and now, by law, have equal employment opportunities and exercise those rights. The law has also recognized that fathers are parents, too, and the laws giving a preference for custodial care to one parent over the other have been eliminated. This has been helpful for children, who now have the opportunity to grow up with both parents, even though they are divorced. It also has increased the volume of custody disputes and brought full employment to counselors, psychologists, and psychiatrists.

In rare but fascinating cases, the court will find that it is in the best interests of the children to live with someone other than either parent. These are rare cases; in most instances courts bend over backward to place children with a natural parent, notwithstanding that one parent has killed the other parent or stolen someone's life savings.

In one recent case, for example, the judge ruled that neither mother nor father were suitable parents. Both were heavy cocaine users and earned too little money to support their habit, much less their children. The judge awarded custody to the grandparents. In an even more unusual case, Kevin Thomas of Van Nuys, California, was granted primary custody of five-year-old Courtney Thomas in July of 1993 by a Los Angeles Superior Court judge. What made the case unusual is that Kevin is not the biological father of Courtney. He was a friend of the biological mother but never lived with her, nor did he have sexual relations with her.

According to the decision, Thomas was totally committed to Courtney. He was involved in the daily care and education of the child—feeding her, clothing her, taking her to and from day care. The judge concluded he was the better custodial parent for the child. The mother, Catherine Thomas, has visitation rights on weekends and holidays.

C. Child Support

Questions of child support, again, involve how much and how long. How much will be determined by the extent of the resources available to each parent to enable that parent to contribute to the child's support. In most jurisdictions it is the lifestyle of the wealthier parent that the child is entitled to have. Thus the principal wage earner's income is critical to the formula used in most states in their efforts to comply with federally mandated guidelines for uniform standards in awards of child support.

In some jurisdictions, the following formula applies to the first $80,000 of income the principal income earner earns per year and above that it's up to the judge:

> 17 percent of the income earner's salary for one child
> 25 percent for two children
> 29 percent for three children
> Up to 35 percent for a maximum of five children

The obligation of both parents is to support their children until the children reach the age of majority, in most jurisdictions eighteen, or in some twenty-one. However, the parent with custody of the children may try to bargain for support beyond age eighteen for college expenses. It is generally not in the mother's best interest to bargain away something that she would otherwise be entitled to, such as child support after the age of majority. Her better strategy is to promote the relationship between father and child so the father will *want* to pay for the child's college education. This strategy is a win-win situation for all involved, particularly the children.

D. Division of Property

In this phase of the trial, the approach is once again fairly standardized. Community property jurisdictions, in most cases, mandate an equal division of the property. (Community property jurisdictions are the states of Arizona, California, Idaho, Louisiana, Nevada, New Mexico, Texas, Washington, and Wisconsin, and the Commonwealth of Puerto Rico.) In other jurisdictions property is generally divided in an equitable if not precisely equal manner. The questions to be resolved are what constitutes the marital property and how much is it worth. Simply put, the marital property is all the property the spouses have acquired during the marriage. The exceptions are property each of them brought to the marriage, but kept as separate, and gifts and inheritances each received during the marriage that they kept separate.

This part of the divorce trial is often the most acrimonious, with allegations regarding oral promises and representations flying back and forth between the spouses. If you doubted what we said earlier that marriage is about love and divorce is about money, you won't doubt it after you see what can go on in the fight over the marital property.

First, there is the argument over the separate property that was brought into the marriage or received as a gift or inheritance after the marriage. The basic concept is that in order to maintain this property as separate property, it must have remained separate, in the name of only the owner of the property, or if cash in an account, only accessible to the spouse claiming the property as separate. If separate property has been commingled with the marital property, it is deemed to be part of the joint property. For example, assume you receive a $1,000 inheritance during your marriage and you deposit it in the joint bank account you have with your husband; it is regarded as a gift from you to the marital property, and it becomes part of your joint assets. An exception to that may be the contribution of your separate property to the acquisition or improvement of real property, where in some jurisdictions you are entitled to a return of your separate property on dissolution of the marriage.

After consideration of what property is *not* the marital property, there is the question of what *is* the marital property. The issue of identification of the marital property, locating it and evaluating it, is more complex than it sounds. The status of the marital property is determined by what is owned by the parties as of the date of separation, adjusted by what happens to the property after the date of separation. For example, suppose your husband is an accountant running his own business. As of the date of separation, that accountancy business, whether in corporate form or run as a sole proprietorship, consists of assets and liabilities that are joint or community assets and liabilities. After the date of separation, that changes to the extent that the separated accountant spouse continues to work at the business using his personal efforts, which, in some jurisdictions, now are his separate efforts. Thus the trick is to allocate any increase or decrease in the value of the business to his separate efforts or to the community business.

Sometimes during the discovery process you will find that assets that you thought were there were not there at the date of separation. Assume there was a $10,000 certificate of deposit in existence in the year before separation and it no longer exists at the date of separation. The obvious question: What happened to it? Assume that during the discovery process you have found a receipt for a fur coat that is not yours. You may have discovered a misappropriation of the joint property, which must be reimbursed to the marital estate. Usually these misappropriations are not quite so blatant, but the use of joint funds to further an illicit relationship during marriage should result in a reimbursement to the joint property.

E. Validity of the Prenuptial Agreement

The issue of the validity of a premarital agreement is often the subject of a trial court decision. Generally, the decision on the validity of the agreement will be determinative of other issues relating to the identification of community property. Thus, you and your lawyer may wish to obtain a determination on the validity of the agreement prior to trial on other issues. Indeed, the outcome of this issue may make other issues moot or may make settlement of the remaining issues easier.

Assuming you are attempting to invalidate the premarital agreement, this trial will be of critical importance to you, and all that we have said in this and the previous chapter applies to your demeanor, your dress, and most important, your own ability to convince the trier of fact that you are an honest and credible witness who is to be believed.

F. The Critical Issue of Date of Separation

The exact date that you and your spouse separated is often an issue that defies settlement and therefore must be tried in a court. The decision on this issue, like the validity of the premarital agreement, will have an impact on other issues, particularly in jurisdictions where the accumulation of marital property ends with the date of separation. The issue arises where, after separation, a spouse continues to contribute from his now separate property earnings to a pension plan. Or he may start a new business. The question then is whether or not that new business is totally separate property because it was begun after the separation date or is it merely an extension of the community or marital business. Again, get your facts right so that your testimony on this significant issue will carry the day.

V. HOW TO BE A STRONG WITNESS FOR YOUR SIDE

A. Five Pointers That Will Make You a Good Witness for You

Now comes the moment when you are on the witness stand to be questioned by your attorney during direct examination and then by your husband's attorney on cross-examination. Here are the five points you need to remember to impress the court as your own best witness.

1. *Image.* Convey a mature, dignified image by the way you dress and talk, and avoid hostility. The other side wants you to look like a bitch on wheels; don't prove their point. Don't use vulgar language. Don't be sarcastic. Don't argue with your husband's attorney.

2. *Boy Scout motto.* If you have done your homework and have been involved with every phase of your divorce as we have urged you to be, you will live up to the motto of the Boy Scouts: Be Prepared. Know the facts of your case and show the opposition that they are not dealing with some silly, simpering fool. Show them they have a knowledgeable, determined, and competent opponent on their hands.

3. *Ears, mind, and voice.* Listen very carefully to the questions you are asked and make sure you clearly understand what is being asked. If it isn't clear—and some times the opposing attorney will deliberately try to befuddle you with a convoluted, obtuse question so you will panic, look silly, and say something stupid—tell the attorney questioning you it is not clear. "I'm sorry, I don't understand what you are asking. Would you please restate the question?"

Then, take the time to process it in your mind and make sure you know what to say—it may well be something you and your attorney have already talked about, in a dry run in her office. Then answer the question simply and briefly.

4. *Answering only what is asked.* This is a critical point. Answer only the question that is asked. *Do not volunteer information that is not sought.* For example, if the question is something like "When did you meet your husband?" simply give the approximate date and nothing more. Say something like "Memorial Day weekend, 1988." *Do not say,* "We met at a cocaine party at Suzanne Zingo's beach house in Dewey Beach, Delaware, on Memorial Day weekend, 1988, where I was dancing nude between beers."

5. *Alcoholics Anonymous method of answering.* One of the mottos of Alcoholics Anonymous is Easy Does It, and that should be your motto in answering questions from the opposing lawyer on cross-examination. *Do not answer quickly.* As your husband's lawyer is questioning you, your lawyer is monitoring the cross-examination to protect you from objectionable questions. So your lawyer has to hear the question and instantly decide whether an objection is appropriate. If you should answer the question without objection, he or she will say nothing, but if the question is objectionable, your attorney will state the objection, the other side may respond, and the judge will rule.

Give your attorney a little time to object. Listen to the question, wait a few beats while you think about the question and while your lawyer decides whether or not to object. Then, if there is no objection, answer the question.

B. General Questions to Discuss with Your Attorney

Here are some odds and ends you may need to discuss with your attorney prior to the trial:

1. *Will you resume use of your maiden name?* If you want to resume using your maiden name, ask that that be a part of the order of dissolution. Even if you don't arrange for this during the trial, most states allow you to file a petition with the court later to resume use of your maiden name. (As a point of information, you may use your maiden name or any name you wish without a court order so long as it is not done to defraud creditors.)

2. *When will the divorce be final?* The date for the finalization of a divorce varies from state to state. Remember the dissolution of your marriage concerns your marital status. The other issues can be separated from that. Usually the judge *does not* rule on the case

immediately upon the conclusion of the trial. The ruling or intended ruling may be handed down some days or weeks later; your attorney will be notified, and in turn she will notify you. At that point you and your attorney will decide the next procedural step. Is the judgment such that you would consider an appeal? Is the judgment clear, or will it require clarification by the judge in a further statement of decision? Assuming the judgment resolves all issues, then comes the work of wrapping up the details of the divorce, the division of property, and the custody questions. We deal with that in a later chapter.

3. *Who will be responsible for seeing that the judgment is properly recorded?* Normally, when the papers granting a decree of divorce are issued, they are sent to your attorney. If you are in a jurisdiction that requires recordation of the decree, your attorney will see that the judgment is recorded, so that the world is on notice that you and your husband are legally divorced and where appropriate what your respective obligations are. It is in your best interests to insist that your attorney send you some proof that the judgment or an abstract of the judgment has been recorded. Some attorneys may hold onto the divorce decree and fail to record it with the county recorder pending your payment of all outstanding fees. Or sometimes your attorney's office is too busy or possibly too inept to do it promptly because it is not as pressing as another client's pending divorce trial.

So to protect yourself, check with the county recorder yourself to make sure the papers have been recorded. Remember, it is your duty to participate in the divorce, and that means through the wrap-up of the entire matter. Others will not protect you or take care of you— you must do it yourself and assure yourself that others do what they are supposed to do. It is, after all, your life; to a busy document clerk, yours is just another case.

In many jurisdictions no such recordation is required. The entry of the judgment on the court's register of actions is sufficient. This entry is the duty of the clerk of the county court.

4. *Are restraining orders needed?* Be sure that your attorney has all restraining orders against your spouse extended and made permanent if the orders still are necessary. If there is any doubt in your mind that your now ex-husband will not leave you alone, continue the restraining order that you had in place since the beginning of the action. We have already reviewed some of the practical problems of

such orders. If a spouse wants to ignore a court order to leave you alone, he probably will ignore it. Again, you have the primary responsibility for your own safety and that of your children and dependents. However, the police will be in a much better position to help you if you have a court order, a copy of which, incidentally, you should carry with you.

VI. HELPFUL WORDS AND PHRASES

Again, there are some words and phrases that will come up at the trial that you should know the meaning of so you can understand and participate more fully.

Objections to questions or *motions to strike answers.* The attorney for either side can raise objections to the questions asked by the other side. Typically, when you are a witness your attorney will question you, during which time your husband's attorney can object to the questions or move to strike your answers. Then your husband's attorney will cross-examine you and your attorney may object to some of the questions asked.

Here are some of the typical objections one side or the other might raise while you are testifying:

1. *No foundation.* Every line of question must have what is called a foundation in law. For example, before you can say what your husband said and did at Thanksgiving dinner last year, you have to establish that there was a Thanksgiving dinner last year and that the two of you were together at Thanksgiving dinner last year. Then you can talk about what was said and done in your presence, assuming you are not running afoul of the hearsay rules.

2. *Argumentative.* Sometimes your husband's attorney will attempt to argue with you on the stand. His objective is not to obtain information from you—which, in theory, is why you are being questioned—but to fluster you or to make a point with the judge. When the opposing attorney says something like "Really, Mrs. Jones, do you expect this court to believe that?" you know he is not eliciting information but rather inciting an argument.

3. *Irrelevant.* An objection on the grounds of relevance tells the judge that your attorney thinks that the question does not have a bearing on the legal questions to be decided by the court. It might be juicy gossip, but it has nothing to do with the case.

4. *Hearsay*. Generally you can only testify to what you personally know and have experienced. What other people have told you or what you have heard them say or events to which you have not been witness is called hearsay. Indeed, any out-of-court statement used to prove the truth of the matter stated is hearsay. Usually hearsay evidence is not accepted as evidence unless it falls within one of the many exceptions to the hearsay rule.

VII. TRIAL SECRETS YOU SHOULD KNOW BUT NOBODY TELLS YOU

Even though the trial procedure is spelled out for you by your attorney and in this book, and you believe you understand the drill, there are not-so-obvious factors that have a significant influence on your life that no one has thought to tell you. We'll deal with some of those things here.

A. Key Influence in Child Custody

We emphasize still one more time that courts all over the country are jammed with cases and are grasping for ways to cope with tremendous caseloads. One of the more common ways is to shunt some of the preliminary work away from the courts and judges while leaving the final decisions with the judge.

Child custody is one of those situations as we have noted earlier. In California the parties to a custody dispute are required to attend at least one session with a trained counselor to attempt to resolve the custody issues. In about 50 percent of the cases this results in an agreement of the parties. In many courts the custody decision may be referred out by the court for a workup by a professional psychologist or psychiatrist who will make a recommendation. This may be a trained child psychologist or licensed social worker or perhaps a psychiatrist. Many courts have panels of psychologists and psychiatrists who devote their practices to court work involving children and custody. The levels of education and experience of these individuals vary widely around the country and often include people who are just starting out in their chosen profession and haven't been doing it long enough to establish their own practice. Thus, the parents who are going through one of the most traumatic events of their lives may not be getting the best help to resolve their problems. Also, some evaluators who work directly for the courts are judged by their production quota—that is, by the number of custody cases they settle in a given time. These evaluators often push to achieve a settlement of the custody issues and move on to the next case. They are more interested in the number of cases they handle than in how well they are handled. Be wary of this, and do not be afraid to complain about it to the administrator of the court if necessary.

Some tips when meeting with an evaluator: Don't try to use the child as a weapon for attacking the other parent, and don't ask the child to say nasty things about the other parent. The child will hate it, and the evaluator will fault you. Each parent should be concerned about asking the child to testify, and in no event should any child be compelled to give testimony against one or the other parent unless it has to do with the child's safety and welfare.

Always refer to the child as "our" child and not "my" child. Make it clear that you understand that while the two spouses are going to terminate their relationship as husband and wife, they will continue to be mother and father. Assure the evaluator that you know the importance to a child of both mother and father in his or her life, and try to convince the evaluator that you want to foster that mutual relationship as much as possible.

The smart evaluator will look for each party's hidden agenda. If either of you wants primary custody of the child so you can hurt the other parent, the evaluator will detect that hidden agenda. Or if either of you wants the child because it means more money, that, too, is often evident.

The Solomon approach is best. When two women came with a baby to Solomon, each claiming to be the mother, Solomon decreed that the baby should be cut in half and divided between the two women. One woman screamed, "No, give the child to the other woman." Solomon knew that the woman who was willing to give the child away was the real mother, who would sacrifice custody to protect her baby. You must convince the evaluator that your only concern is for the best interests of the child, and, while you want custody, it is only because you believe that would be in the best interest of the child.

Finally, be sure that your attorney is present when the evaluator presents his or her findings to the judge. This is critically important.

B. The New Mate Factor

People being people, after a bad marriage and a painful divorce, you or your husband may make another romantic connection and remarry or have a live-in mate. It happens all the time.

When it happens, it introduces the "New Mate Factor." If there are children, the new mate will soon have opinions about the relationships with those children and relationships with the ex-spouse. This will usually create some tension. However, the tension about children and custody is nothing compared to the tension over money.

We mentioned before that the ruling on alimony may be that it continues for a certain period of time or until the supported ex-spouse remarries, whichever occurs first. As we noted before, this invites the supported ex-spouse to refrain from a new legal marriage. That doesn't stop the supported spouse from living with a new lover while cashing the alimony checks. This also prompts the alimony-paying ex-spouse to hire detectives, obtain photos and tapes, and go back to court to contest the amount of alimony or to terminate it entirely. In some states there are specific statutes to deal with this issue. In California, for example, the contribution of a cohabitor to reduce the supported spouse's expenses may be considered in a reduction of alimony, and may create a presumption of decreased need. However, the law is in a state of change on this issue, and the better tactic is to obtain an agreement at the time of settlement about the effect of a live-in lover. In some cases you may want to bargain for an incentive to remarry, particularly if you plan on doing so anyway, such as the payment of $50,000 if the remarriage occurs within three years. There are any number of variations on this theme.

On the other hand, if the new mate is the mate of the spouse paying support, she will quickly become irritated with the need to make alimony payments. That's because her lover or husband is mandated to use money otherwise available for their new joint lifestyle to pay an ex-spouse who contributes nothing to their new happiness.

Another complicating problem that can force a crisis is whether or not the new mate's income is to be included in the calculation of child support. The law on this issue is likewise in a state of flux, but the emotional pressures are constant. What new spouse wants to work an eight-hour day five days a week to support someone else's kids? Prior to marriage this obligation may have been easily ignored, but when it is coming out of the new mate's pocket, it can create some horrendous problems at home. We know, for example, of one case where a husband, a doctor with a good medical practice, remarried and the ex-wife went after his new wife's pension fund, bonuses, and profit-sharing account as resources to reduce the ex-husband's expenses, causing him to have more money available to him that he otherwise would not have had. The result, in this case, was a vicious and expensive retrying of some of the divorce issues. Old hatreds were revived, and the ex-spouse doctor finally threw up his hands and closed down his practice so there was no money coming in to pay the alimony or child support. That conduct might not be acceptable in all jurisdictions. A spouse who closes down a business or quits a job to avoid support payments is likely to find himself in hot water with the court.

In most jurisdictions a parent invites jail time for simply closing down a business or quitting a job to avoid paying court-ordered child support. In addition, a support order that is not modified continues to accrue at the rate ordered, accumulates interest, and will in time be collected. It can be collected from whatever the supporting party is using to survive.

C. Kamikaze Attack on Alimony and Child Support

While it is difficult to believe that a paying spouse would quit a job or shut down a business, the avoidance of paying support is a strong incentive to do just that. Without exploring the psychology or the motives involved, we can say that there are cases where the husband, ordered to pay spousal and child support, deliberately stops earning money. Please do not ask us what kind of man would want to deprive his own children of food, clothing, and shelter. Some men and, presumably some women, too, would rather sabotage their own income and the security of their children to abrogate their duty to pay alimony and child support.

This is done in a variety of ways; one possibility is in refusing to accept raises and bonuses, sometimes with the tacit understanding that these monies will be made available to them later, after you have remarried, or after jurisdiction to award spousal support has terminated. This, of course, may require the employer to lie in court under oath. While it is difficult to believe that an employer would run the risk of lying under oath, it is done particularly in situations where the employer is a relative of the husband or a longtime friend.

It is relatively easy for an owner of a business to hide his income and quite difficult to catch him at it. He may have two or maybe even three sets of books. The accountant will nearly always cooperate with the husband's efforts to hide money. If you have the resources, you may discover this by monitoring your husband's lifestyle. Is he driving a Ferrari and does his new friend wear mink? A man who pleads that his business is barely breaking even will have a considerable amount of explaining to do in court if he is taking European vacations and living in a multimillion-dollar mansion while claiming an inability to pay spousal or child support.

Until recent years the threat to declare bankruptcy was generally only that, a threat. In these more difficult economic times, small businesses are going into bankruptcy at the rate of hundreds per day. However, orders for child and spousal support cannot be discharged in bankruptcy. That means that what he owes you prior to filing a petition in bankruptcy he will still owe you, despite the bankruptcy. Your problem is collecting it, but at least the amount of support accrued while the order is in effect will always be hanging over his head. Although bankruptcy stays all other court proceedings, including your divorce action, the stay may be lifted upon order from the bankruptcy court, and your husband may attempt to modify the family law court order for support to reduce or terminate it entirely. Remember, your spouse is living on something. You need to find out what that is and secure your share of it.

The supporting spouse may attempt to eliminate his obligation by quitting his job or getting fired. He may quit one job and take a low-paying job allowing him just barely to survive. Another tactic is for the supporting spouse simply to dump his job and his life and flee to another state or country. Unless he deliberately changes his identity, which he very well might, there are laws in the United States to help you find him and to attempt to enforce the support orders for your children. District attorneys throughout the country are making a concerted effort to find and collect support from these deadbeat dads. The problem is that DAs are inundated with these cases, and it is a time-consuming effort.

There have been several recent California cases that hold that a support-paying spouse cannot abrogate his obligation simply by giving up his well-paying job and, for example, going back to school. However, there is one case that allowed a supporting spouse to enter a seminary and relieved him of his spousal support obligation. In that case the ex-husband was able to show that he had made arrangements to satisfy his child support obligations and that his former spouse was capable of supporting herself. Unusual circumstances, indeed.

Your recourse in such situations is to bring your ex-spouse back into court and prove that he is deliberately hiding income or that his motive for changing jobs is simply to undermine your right to support. This, of course, will require a trial. It is expensive and will nearly always result in some reduction of your court-ordered support.

If there is a way to bond against his failure to pay support, such as through establishment of a trust or through the purchase of an annuity from which support will be paid by the third-party annuity holder, you should explore that possibility. The down side: That requires that your ex have the funds to purchase the annuity or provide other security for payment. Let's assume that your ex-husband has a residence. He can be ordered to place his residence in trust as security for payment of support. Or upon default in payments, you can execute on the judgment and bring foreclosure proceedings against his house. Make sure, of course, that there is sufficient equity in the house to make this rather expensive process worthwhile.

D. Reservation of Jurisdiction

The use of the device of reserving jurisdiction is often used when the issue of the status of the marriage—that is, whether you are married or divorced—is bifurcated from the other issues. The court may grant the dissolution of the marriage and reserve all other issues for later decision. These other issues are usually the issues relating to property division. It would be unusual for a divorce to be granted where temporary support issues have not been resolved.

E. The Effect on Your Money of Children Who Are Not Yours

Another complicating factor arises when your ex-spouse remarries and has more children by the new spouse or marries a person with children from another marriage who are brought into the union.

This will obviously put a strain on the income stream of the alimony and child support payer and put pressure on him to apply to the court for lower payments to you. In most jurisdictions a parent cannot undercut his obligation for the support of his children by making or acquiring other children.

F. Tax and Term of Alimony

You should know that the monies your ex-spouse pays you as spousal support is income tax deductible for him and taxable to you. So when you are calculating your expenses, allow sufficient money to pay the tax on the alimony you will receive.

The question of the length of time your ex-spouse will be obligated to pay alimony is, in most states, related to the length of your marriage. As a rule of thumb, a marriage that has endured for ten years is considered a long-term relationship, and alimony is often granted for an indefinite period.

In order for a court to legitimately provide for a reduction or cessation of support at a future date, there must be some showing in the evidence that at some future date the wife will be able to support herself. Often, if the dissolution involves a relatively young wife in an eight- to twelve-year marriage, the court may set a return date for the reconsideration of the support order. Or the court may order support for a period of time, giving the supported spouse the opportunity to come into court and obtain an extension of the order. Often, nonworking spouses who can but don't work are warned at the time of the initial hearing that they will be expected to help to support themselves. Unfortunately, the liberation of women has resulted in some rather sad orders for spousal support for women in their forties and fifties who grew up in a generation where women were not expected to have careers other than the raising of children and providing a home to the wage earner. We hope that the early chapters in this book urging you to be prepared to provide for yourself before marriage will have some impact on this generation of brides.

CHAPTER THIRTEEN

The Ending

IN THIS CHAPTER YOU WILL LEARN WHAT YOU HAVE TO DO AT THE END OF THE DIVORCE TRIAL:

> I. Possible outcomes and your alternatives
> II. The marriage is dead—and now the funeral arrangements
> III. Some words you should know
> IV. Some pitfalls to beware of falling into

I. POSSIBLE OUTCOMES AND YOUR ALTERNATIVES

After the filing of the complaint, the depositions and the discovery, the interviews, the sleuthing and gathering of evidence, the settlement or the trial, it is suddenly over. Everything that could be said has been said and it is in the hands of the judge. Sometimes—infrequently—the judge will render her verdict from the bench at the end of the trial. More frequently, she will review the transcript of the trial, the exhibits, her notes on the testimony and demeanor of the husband, wife, and other witnesses to see who is the most credible, the lawyers' arguments, and then, finally, will render a written judgment, usually within a few weeks of taking the case under submission. In some states there are penalties when judges delay in making their decisions; for example, in California the judgment must be rendered within ninety days of the submission of the matter (after all the evidence is in and the arguments concluded).

It is an anxiety-producing phone call when you are told that the final decision is completed and waiting for you to come into the office to review. This decision will affect your life for some years to come. It will often decide the custody of the children, who gets what property from the marriage, and the terms of much of your immediately foreseeable life. Once you have the written decision, it is common to read it along with your attorney so she can interpret and explain any part that is not clear to you.

In some jurisdictions before the final judgment is entered by the court, the judge will prepare an intended or tentative decision, and that will be sent to your attorney. One of the attorneys will be directed to prepare a statement of decision and judgment based on the tentative decision. The parties are given the opportunity to object to the statement of decision or to seek clarification or augmentation of the decision before it is finalized into a judgment. There are certain time restrictions for accomplishing this.

In other jurisdictions the judge will provide findings of fact and conclusions of law based on those findings of fact. Again, the attorney may seek clarification or augmentation or may even attempt to obtain a new hearing on certain issues.

Whether it is a statement of decision or findings and conclusions, this judgment is intended to decide all issues that have been placed before the judge for decision.

Sometimes one of the spouses will ask for a gag order on the terms of the judgment. This issue of whether a gag order—or, in effect, an order sealing the file—will be granted is a matter requiring a hearing and ruling by the court. That decision will be based on the extent to which the publicity is likely to impact the minor children of the parties. Otherwise, cases decided in the public system are in the public domain for all to see.

YOGI BERRA WAS RIGHT ABOUT BASEBALL AND DIVORCE

The famous baseball catcher Yogi Berra was noted for his quaint observations about baseball and life, and one that applies to both baseball and divorce is that "It ain't over until it's over." One big secret about divorce is that it often is never over. You may be going back to renegotiate for modification of the terms of the divorce many times after the final decree is awarded. The key is "changed circumstances." When the circumstances of either party's life change, often that party wants a change in the alimony, child support, visitation rights, or custody arrangement. One side's failure to pay or obey an order may result in a return to court. Because all of our lives change, this is probably unavoidable, and you are back at the negotiation table or in front of the judge again. Or, as Yogi would say, "It's déjà vu all over again."

Most people approach a court case feeling that they will either win or lose. Experienced lawyers and judges, however, know that a case has been fairly resolved when neither side is entirely happy with the outcome. The theory seems to be that a reasonable compromise is better than an outright, complete victory or defeat.

However you feel when you receive the final written decision, you will either accept it as satisfactory to you or you will decide it is not something with which you can live. Obviously, if it is satisfactory, you need only carry out the provisions of the order and get on with your life.

If, however, you decide that the judge's decision about the terms of the divorce, the custody, and property division are not satisfactory, you have two alternatives. One is to grit your teeth and live with the decision and the other is to appeal the decision to a higher court.

A. Thinking About Appealing the Ruling

Putting aside the question of the legal grounds of appeal, you may want to weigh several other personal factors before you begin the appeal process.

1. *Effect on you.* An appeal generally takes from two years, at the very best, to as long as five years to process. During that time your life is unsettled. If you are successful on the appeal, that may mean that the judgment is reversed and it is sent back down to the trial court for a new trial at least on those issues which were reversed. (And remember, in family law each issue tends to interact with others, so while you may appeal on some issues that you think the court decided incorrectly, your ex-husband may find himself forced to appeal some issues with which you were satisfied because of the possible effect a reversal would have on these favorable issues.)

Will you be emotionally and mentally prepared to go through another trial, with discovery, depositions, and court hearings all over again? And remember, if the case is reversed, it almost always goes back on remand to the same judge, although with instructions regarding rectification of the mistake the judge has made.

It is time for a reality check and an honest evaluation of your motivation in filing an appeal. Ask yourself if a substantial part of your motivation is to prolong the agony for your former spouse, who has begun to get on with his life. There are some spouses who don't want to let go; these folks, both men and women, are willing to dig in and fight simply to remain in contact with the spouse they claim to hate. Is the revenge factor your principal motivating factor? If your primary goal throughout the divorce was vengeance and the court's judgment did not give you satisfaction on that score, you will not get it on appeal.

2. *Effect on others.* What will be the effect on the children and your ex-spouse if you go through a replay of the first divorce proceedings by fighting over the terms of the divorce ruling?

3. *Who will be your attorney?* Is your present attorney willing to file and carry forward the appeal for you, or will you have to find another attorney and, in some ways, start from scratch with parts of the case? What does your attorney recommend? What does your present attorney think of your chances of success on an appeal? Your present attorney knows more about the details of your case than any other attorney at that moment and probably can give you the best legal assessment of the odds of your success on appeal.

4. *Cost vs. benefit analysis.* Look at an appeal from a strictly business viewpoint. It is going to cost you money to take the appeal; what

are the benefits you will reap from the appeal even if you win? It may be that the potential for benefit is great for you and the cost relatively low. If that is the case, it may make sense to go for the appeal. However, if the cost comes close to what you might gain, it probably is not worth the aggravation, time, additional pain, and the risk of losing.

B. The Legal Grounds for Appeal

The legal grounds for appeal are quite limited, particularly in the family law area. The principal question to be considered by the appellate court is whether the trial court abused its discretion in making the rulings it made. For example, in a state that has an equal division of property rule, and the property you received was less in value than that received by your spouse, there may have been an abuse of discretion. But remember, the trial court will hear from your witnesses and from your husband's witnesses. It is generally not considered an abuse of discretion for the trial court to choose a value based on the testimony of one expert or another or to pick a value in between so long as the decision has a legal grounding and a basis in the facts presented.

Another example of an abuse of discretion is found in cases when the court orders a termination of support after a long marriage where there is no evidence that the supported spouse can support herself. An appeal may be justified to address an issue on which there are conflicting appellate decisions or in the event the trial court judge has erroneously applied the law to your facts.

Remember, all facts on appeal are assumed to have been resolved in favor of the nonappealing party, the respondent on appeal. The burden is on the apellant, and it is a heavy burden to sustain.

You may also use the filing of notice of appeal as a bargaining chip to force your husband to stipulate to a change in the judgment. He may not want to undertake the expense and pressure of an appeal and may be willing to negotiate. But you must be very sure of the validity of your appeal. After all, you and your husband do not have a good track record for negotiations if you've gone through a trial. The possibility that you have to pay your spouse's attorney fees if your appeal is without merit is another factor to weigh.

C. Difference Between Appeal and Petition for Modification

An appeal is taken to a different and higher court seeking to change some significant aspect of the trial judge's ruling. A modification, in contrast, leaves the original judge's orders in place, except for the modification. This is dealt with at the trial court level, not by appeal to a higher court. For example, assume that since the trial court's judgment, the supporting spouse may have been fired or suffered a physical ailment that makes it no longer practical or possible for him or her to pay the amount of support the court ordered. Or the payer may have received a substantial raise or bonus. The recipient of support may petition the court for an increase if she was awarded an amount of spousal support insufficient to meet the marital standard of living. A caution: Do not believe that every time your former husband gets a raise you will be entitled to an increase in spousal support. The court expects that you will begin to support yourself by entering the job market and enjoying raises of your own. Child support, on the other hand, in most jurisdictions tracks the higher earning parent's standard of living. So the court may be petitioned to modify the amount of the child support.

Any part of the final divorce decree that is subject to modification can be the subject of a petition for modification. However, usually the only parts of a judgment that are modifiable are those relating to child and spousal support. Do not suffer from the delusion that you can seek a modification of the property division years or even months after the decree. In fact, it is under only very unusual circumstances that a modification of provisions other than support can occur.

We strongly warn against your failing to obey the court orders while the modification petition or appeal is pending. You can get yourself in a pile of trouble by ceasing court-ordered payments. The court order remains in effect until it is paid or changed. Thus, any defaulted payments continue to accrue—in some jurisdictions, with high interest rates.

Most states strictly enforce court-ordered support and, more often, are beginning to make an example of those who fail to pay by ordering jail time for them. This has been applied to delinquent fathers and ex-husbands, but expect it to apply equally to delinquent mothers and ex-wives as they become the wage earners in more families. Another enforcement program is known as the tax intercept program, which is nationwide and which intercepts tax refunds paid to delinquent support payers.

D. Summary of Pointers If You Decide to Appeal

1. *Act quickly.* In most states appeals must be filed promptly—often within thirty to sixty days of the final written decision being handed down. Thus, if the notice is delayed in the mail, and you aren't notified for a few days and take your time reading the written decision and a few more days waiting to see your attorney, you may only have a few days left to file your appeal. These time limitations on appeal exist partially because the courts prefer to see fewer cases appealed. Appeals are disfavored in the interest of early and final resolution, especially in family law cases. If you have decided to appeal but you file your notice of appeal after the last day for filing, you have no recourse. The date that the notice of appeal must be filed is jurisdictional, meaning that the court loses jurisdiction to consider your appeal if it is not filed by the last day set by statute for filing. So do not delay thinking that one more day won't make a difference. It does.

2. *Stay with your present attorney.* Unless there is a real problem, if your trial attorney feels she can handle an appeal, you are usually better off staying with your trial attorney for the appeal. Of course, you may feel he or she is the one who failed to get you the results you wanted and thought you deserved. If you do not have faith in your present attorney, by all means bail out and get another one. There are lawyers who specialize in appeals. However, keep in mind that you have very little time to act, and you have to move quickly to meet the deadline for filing your notice of appeal.

3. *Prepare the appeal at start of trial.* Appeals are best prepared from the beginning of the trial. That may sound strange because you will not decide to take an appeal until the trial is over. You and your attorney should go into the divorce trial on the assumption that there may be mistakes made by the trial court that result in an outcome you may not like, thus leading to an appeal on your part. In order to preserve your rights on appeal, your attorney must, on the court record, object to all evidence or procedures that are improper or inappropriate. Even if the judge overrules the objections, they are on the record and the appellate judge will see the possible judicial errors. These errors will suggest that the trial judge's rulings, based on these judicial errors, may have been wrong on facts or points of law. If your attorney fails to object at the trial level, you will have waived that right and you may not raise it for the first time on

appeal. You need this foundation to make a case on appeal for overturning the trial judge's decisions that you feel were incorrect or prejudiced against you.

4. *Obey the original ruling while appeal is pending.* It is important while appealing any part of the original decision of the judge that you obey the terms of the divorce decree until the appeal is concluded. If you seem to be a scofflaw ignoring— even temporarily— the rulings of one judge, not only will your failure to comply adversely impact your case, but in most cases your failure to obey the orders of the lower court will result in legal sanctions against you. There may be occasions when to obey the orders of the trial court would moot the appeal. Still, you need a court order allowing you to suspend your performance.

5. *In some cases, get a stay of execution.* If it is a hardship or you have serious difficulty obeying the trial court's judgment pending appeal—for example, it may be that you are appealing a custody ruling giving care and control of the children to a husband you believe will abuse them—you can file for an immediate, temporary stay of execution of the trial court's order. This, if granted, will delay the implementation of the judge's order on that issue until the appeal is ruled upon. You may have to post a bond by paying a premium in order to stay monetary orders.

6. *The appellant has the burden of proof on the appeal.*

    a.   Error in interpreting the law. Judges can make mistakes in interpreting the law. Or it may be that the judge failed to consider all the appropriate law or prior cases on the particular issue. Thus, the trial court's ruling cannot be sustained on appeal and requires correction either in the appellate court or in a new trial after remand to the trial court.

    b.   Error in weighing the facts. It may be that the judge didn't consider all the facts or didn't understand all the facts in the case. He or she may have misunderstood some of the evidence or testimony or misinterpreted it. This is a heavy burden to sustain on appeal.

    c.   Demonstrated prejudice. If you can show genuine bias against you by the trial court—whether it be because of your gender, background, race, or politics—you may have a basis for appeal. This type of prejudice as a ground for appeal is, incidentally, extremely difficult to establish.

d. Miscalculation. The judge may have understood the law and understood the facts, but that understanding resulted in an erroneous calculation. Suppose the judge based the alimony, child support, or property division on an error in math that led him to conclude there was more or less income and property than there really is. This could be relatively easy to demonstrate, and it is also relatively rare that it happens, but there is the possibility. If there is such an unintentional error, that should be addressed by a motion in the trial court or in working through the intended decision prior to entry of the judgment. If certain property was overlooked in the trial court, such after-discovered property is always subject to the jurisdiction of the trial court for division at a later time.

APPEALS THAT SHOW HOW BIZARRE IT CAN GET

Often appeals of divorce rulings can take unusual twists, resulting in unusual cases and outcomes. We talk about some of the more notorious here to illustrate the point and because celebrity cases are reported when equally strange private-party cases are not. In any event, consider the twists divorce ruling appeals have taken in these cases.

The story of the Henry and Hedi Kravis divorce settlement that she later appealed is detailed in Sarah Bartlett's book *The Money Machine*. Here is how the divorce settlement was originally crafted, ending Henry's marriage to Hedi: Henry and Hedi signed a separation agreement ending their marriage in 1983. Henry agreed to give Hedi 30 percent of his stake—valued the year before at $7.2 million—in companies that his firm, Kohlberg Kravis Roberts, owned. She would receive a minimum of $3 million and a maximum of $4 million under this agreement. The ink was barely dry on the settlement when KKR started doing mega-leveraged buy-out deals, and Kravis's fortune skyrocketed into the hundreds of millions. Off to court Hedi went, charging that Henry had defrauded her. According to the 1989 decision handed down by Acting State Supreme Court Justice Walter Schackman, Henry's former partner, Jerome Kohlberg, "supposedly" told her that her ex-husband had understated the true value of his holdings in 1982 by about $10 million. But her case was dismissed, with Judge Schackman observing that her separation document had been drafted over a three-year period by lawyers of her own choosing. She "had the means and opportunity to investigate the true nature of [the] defendant's assets, either personally or through her representatives."

So you can see the value of thorough preparation. Divorce trials and appeals and related legal actions can become incredibly complicated.

II. THE MARRIAGE IS DEAD—AND NOW THE FUNERAL ARRANGEMENTS: A DIVORCE CONCLUSION CHECKLIST

A. The Final Decree

As we noted above, obtain a copy of the judgment as soon as it is available. Review it carefully with your attorney to be sure that you understand all the terms of the judgment, particularly what your responsibilities are as well as the obligations of your ex-husband.

B. Cash, Precious Metals, Coins, Stamps, Gems, Etc.

If there is cash or other portable precious items that are to be divided with your spouse, making the exchange in the presence of a third-party witness such as your attorney and the exchange of mutual receipts will reduce later recrimination and accusations.

C. Exchange of Property: Real Estate, Vehicles, Etc.

Property such as real estate, vehicles, stocks, bonds, bank accounts, trust accounts, income property, property owned by the family business, and the like requires both sides to sign releases and transfer documents and other papers. In most cases, these need to be recorded with either the county recorder or with the Department of Motor Vehicles.

D. Income Tax

While the parties are married but separated, it may be necessary to consider the filing of joint income tax returns, particularly if the separation spans a new tax year. Federal and state tax returns (where applicable) must be prepared and signed by both parties and filed with the appropriate agency. Be sure to get a copy of the return to be filed well before the deadline so your accountant can review it. Consider indemnities from the spouse in control of the income and the reporting of that income.

E. Social Security

To obtain your Social Security benefits, you will need to notify the Social Security Administration when you are coming close to the time of your eligibility. You are eligible for Social Security benefits based on your spouse's employment if your marriage to him lasted more than ten years.

F. Insurance, Financial Records, Trusts, and Wills

Unless the court has ordered that the spouse paying support must maintain insurance for the benefit of the supported spouse, life insurance beneficiaries can and should be changed. Trusts, wills, and deeds must reflect the changed relationship between husband and wife.

G. Charge Accounts and Credit Cards

Creditors need to be notified and informed as to the terms of the judgment regarding responsibility for payments of joint accounts. Be aware that creditors, unless joined as parties to the divorce proceeding, are not bound by the judgment. The nonemployed spouse must obtain her own cards, which she may have trouble accomplishing without the cooperation of her ex-spouse.

See our earlier chapters regarding your preparation for dissolution of your marriage.

H. Identification Papers: Driver's License and Passport

These may have to be reissued if your name has changed. All persons of whatever age must now have individual passports.

I. Payment of Debts

The final divorce decree should indicate who is to pay what debts, but it is wise to notify all creditors, not only credit card companies, of the court order. Again, the divorce decree is not binding on the creditors unless they are parties to the action and, therefore, both spouses remain liable for payment. The best that can be done in this situation is to obtain an indemnity from the obligated spouse as well as security for the payment of the debt.

J. Stolen Property

Personal property that you removed from the possession of your ex-husband, or that he stole from you during the divorce proceedings, should be returned. Realistically, with the resolution of the proceedings some of the bitterness between the two spouses may also resolve, and items of personal property that may have vanished may now be found. You should ask for your property and return that belonging to your husband.

K. Name Change

Returning to your maiden name may be a choice you made during the trial. Some wives prefer to keep their maiden name during marriage or to keep their married name after divorce. Usually the latter is done because the children bear their father's name. Generally, you can use any name you like as long as there is no intent to defraud other people. Of course there are some glitches, such as the infamous case of the married woman in Kentucky who retained her maiden name after marrying. The Kentucky Department of Motor Vehicles refused to issue her a driver's license in her maiden name on the grounds that the person with that name ceased to exist when she got married. Since that case, we think Kentucky has come into the twentieth century and changed that law. However, if you have a problem, you may want to seek more information by contacting the Center for a Woman's Own Name at 261 Kimberly, Barrington, Illinois 60010 ([312] 381-2130).

III. SOME WORDS YOU SHOULD KNOW

Even here, at the end of the process, there are some words and phrases you should understand for your own benefit. They include:

Interlocutory. In some states (Nebraska, Massachusetts, and Utah, for example) the written judgment of the court is not final until a waiting period has passed. This is a last-ditch effort of the state to preserve the marriage in case the two people have second thoughts after the trial. So when the written judgment of the court is handed down after the trial, if the divorce decree is *interlocutory,* that means it doesn't legally take effect until the waiting period is over, and the court may require the filing of another document. In the states mentioned that is six months, except for Utah, where it is three.

Stay of execution. A temporary order of the court that delays the carrying out of a court order. This may occur during an appeal.

Reservation of jurisdiction. Sometimes the judge or the parties wish to defer a decision on some issue until a later time while settling most of the issues of the case. For example, suppose the wage earner becomes incapacitated, and whether or not he or she is going to return to work and a particular income level is uncertain at the time of trial. The judge may issue the divorce decree granting no or minimal alimony, but *reserve jurisdiction* on the point until six months later, when it can be determined if the wage earner has returned to work and is capable of paying support at a different level. The device of reserving jurisdiction is often used when the issue of the status of the marriage—that is, whether you are married or divorced—is bifurcated from the other issues. The court may grant the dissolution of the marriage and reserve all other issues for later decision.

IV. OTHER PITFALLS

A. Lack of Recordation

Be sure that every document that is supposed to be recorded is properly filed and recorded with the county recorder's office and appropriate government agency or private entity. This means that if you are owed money under the judgment you should and must record the judgment or an abstract of the judgment in every county in which your ex-husband has property. This will guarantee that you will get your money before he disposes of any property.

B. Not Protecting Yourself

Remember that love and marriage that turn into divorce also may turn into hatred, so take sensible steps to protect yourself physically, financially, and legally. Recording documents is one way. Reviewing and reinforcing your physical security is another way. If you have the facts to support it, get an injunction against stalking and harassing. Too many ex-wives take the question of security too lightly until it is too late.

C. Vengeance, Wallowing, and Bitterness

Part of repairing your ruptured life is to get busy and begin your new life. You will be depressed, perhaps bitter, and feeling vulnerable. Avoid the continuing quest for vengeance; avoid wallowing in self-pity. Do not date men you would not have been caught dead with before all this happened. Stay away from booze and drugs. This kind of behavior is a temporary and unsatisfactory solution to a permanent problem, and the sooner you are able to embark on a productive and worthwhile life, the better you and those who depend upon you will feel about life.

It is not our business here to provide career or psychological counseling, but we feel constrained—having been with you this long— to comment briefly on the next phase of your life. Recognize that divorce is a major event in your life, but it should be a milestone and not a millstone around your neck. Hopefully, it will open the doors to a better and more fulfilling life for you, and you should go forward with that in your mind.

CHAPTER FOURTEEN

Special Issues

IN THIS CHAPTER YOU WILL LEARN ABOUT
SOME SPECIAL ASPECTS OF DIVORCE THAT YOU
MAY NOT HAVE THOUGHT ABOUT BEFORE:

I. What happens when business partners get a divorce
II. How to protect yourself against stalking and violence
III. What if the alimony or support payments stop
IV. Rules for your personal behavior after a divorce
V. Medical insurance, taxes, and other special
   concerns

I. WHAT HAPPENS WHEN BUSINESS PARTNERS GET A DIVORCE

You have a complicating factor when the two people dissolving their personal relationship are also in business together. It is one thing to split up the household and remove yourself to separate beds, but what about splitting up the factory or the retail store?

Since one of the two ex-spouses may be paying alimony or child support, the other probably doesn't want to do anything that will harm the business that is the source of that money. They may have to continue working together to enable the business to prosper. For example, when Ivana Trump sued Donald to challenge the prenuptial agreement she had signed, the divorce action made Donald's creditors nervous and less willing to extend him loans for his business that could have jeopardized his ability to pay Ivana.

Today, futuristic-thinking directors sitting on corporate boards may require prenuptial agreements and insurance policies to protect the company's financial health in the event one of the key executives becomes involved in a messy and expensive divorce. For years "key man" life insurance has been recognized as essential to business survival on the grounds that if a critical executive died, it would hurt the business. Now that same philosophy is extended to other events of life that might seriously affect a key executive's ability to function, including the period of a divorce. The impact of divorce on businesses is becoming more and more the subject of attention with accounting magazines and business magazines, from *Jewelry's Circular* to *Women's Wear Daily*. We learned from *Women's Wear Daily* of the possibility of the collapse of a major business in the clothing field, the Esprit Corporation, because the two founding partners both responsible for running the business were husband and wife now in the process of divorce.

Here we make reference to businesses in which both spouses actively participate: a hardware store where they work together side by side, a fast-food franchise, or a ranch where both work in the fields. We do not refer to businesses or practices that require one spouse to have special expertise or a license. There the issue of division is easy because there can be none. The spouse with the license gets the business, and the other spouse gets a like share of some other assets or cash.

Difficult decisions have to be made where both spouses work on the farm or ranch that is not capable of division. Sometimes the court will order a sale giving each spouse the right of first refusal. Thus, the fate of the business becomes the subject of a bidding war between the spouses as to who will get the business by paying more for it. An arm's length sale to a third party will serve to set the fair market value of the business, and both may be better off with the cash from the sale. Often, however, a sale of a business in the midst of a divorce may not bring the best price, and the parties are better off attempting to buy out one another. That kind of a deal between spouses may require some creative financing, and it may mean that the departing spouse still maintains an interest in the business, because the promissory note reflecting what is due as her share of the joint business will probably be secured by the business assets.

There are ways of meeting and accommodating some of these problems, but only if the spouses will commit to work together to resolve the issue. That does not always work and sometimes the business goes down the tubes along with the marriage.

II. HOW TO PROTECT YOURSELF AGAINST STALKING AND VIOLENCE

We deal here with the potential harassment that may arise after a divorce. Presumably you have obtained orders against domestic violence early on in the divorce proceeding that have been extended to permanent status. But in some rare instances the violence may not begin until after the divorce, when the grim reality of it stirs incredibly deep, primitive emotions on both sides. We would be remiss if we didn't alert you to the need for protecting yourself against the kind of mindless violence that your divorce might generate for you. Don't hesitate a minute to obtain an order against such violence.

There are books on how to protect yourself, and we have previously cautioned you to obtain stay-away orders or injunctions from the court requiring your ex-husband to leave you alone. However, the cold, hard fact is that *you are pretty much on your own when it comes to protecting yourself—at least at critical times when it matters.*

> My mother, Beth Blackburn, was stalked for eight months by a man who sent her death threats, harassed her at work by phone, and followed her all around town. He knew her every move. She was told by the police that there was nothing they could do to protect her. On April 22, 1993, my mother was murdered in her apartment in Baton Rouge. The man who stalked my mom for eight months and finally murdered her before committing suicide himself was my father.
>
> —Lisa Gallant Norris

The *Christian Science Monitor* reports that there are 200,000 ordinary people—mostly women—who are being beaten, harassed, tortured, and murdered by stalkers every year in the United States. Many of these women are ex-wives and some are ex-girlfriends, but they are all the female half of a broken relationship, and the emotions run high whether it is a broken marriage or a broken romance.

Daily we see newspaper reports on stalkings and violence against women by ex-husbands and ex-boyfriends. Some are bizarre, all are tragic. We know of one case where the estranged husband invaded his wife's apartment, sexually assaulted her, and almost beat her to death. The woman is blind and confined to a wheelchair. In another instance the wife had a job as a public bus driver, and her husband lay in wait for her at a bus stop, boarded the bus, and attacked her. She radioed for help and tried to drive off, but he continued to beat her, she lost control, and the bus crashed, decapitating her estranged husband. In another case the husband shot his ex-wife, condemning her to a wheelchair for life, and fled with their two-year-old child to a foreign country. It was years before he came back and was prosecuted. And only then was the child returned to her disabled mother.

The tragic stories seem almost endless.

The greatest danger to the stalking victim are the illusions she carries in her own mind. For example, there is the illusion that the system—the police, the courts, the law—will protect her. In an ideal world that might happen, but in the reality of the streets the system is too ponderous, too out of date, too timid to do much in time to save the stalking victim.

Jane Smith knows. The system failed her.

Jane married John Smith, and they had a child. Jane claimed that John had been abusive before, and that after the marriage he became violent and never let up on her. When she became pregnant three months after the wedding, she claimed he started sleeping around with other women and punching Jane when he was home. She said he particularly enjoyed slamming his fists into her stomach.

Once while Jane was baby-sitting, John broke into the house, punching his fist through the window and beating her up while the terrified children looked on.

She filed for divorce, but he contested it. She moved to hide from him, but the court gave John visitation rights and told him where Jane lived. She got a court order, designed to protect her, which she claimed he violated nine times without any action by the system.

One day Jane took their child to the market. She found John waiting for her when they came out of the market. He beat her up as six construction workers looked on and did nothing. He stole her keys, and while she was calling the police, went to her apartment and destroyed everything in it. The police came; he threatened to commit suicide and was taken to a mental hospital, from which he was released one month later. Immediately, he returned to her apartment building and lay in wait for her. When she came out, she described the event: "He punched me and knocked me down, jerked me up, took my purse and keys and pulled me down the crosswalk. I was screaming for help. He punched me in the nose. He kicked me and he kicked me and he kicked me—it seems like twenty hours. I was choking, gagging on my own blood. I thought I would die."

The building security guard appeared, but John told him to leave and he did. Jane was finally saved by some neighbors who came to her rescue. Finally, John was arrested, tried for aggravated battery, and sentenced to three years in jail. In the weird arithmetic of our legal system, of course, three years actually means fifteen months. John was released to the streets in April 1993.

Experts tell us that the best defense against a stalking, violent ex-husband is to remove yourself from contact with him as much as possible. Ideally, you should not see him—which, of course, is difficult if there are children and he has visitation rights. The solution would be to move and start your life anew in a different place with a different identity. But if you take the child, you may lose custody. A second solution, less satisfactory if children are to be exchanged for visitation, is to do it in a neutral public place like a mall or park or police station. As judges become more familiar with spousal abuse, they recognize that the batterer should be precluded from contact with the children as well. Thus, at least for a time, you may, on paper, avoid all contact with the abuser.

The places where you live and work should have security, such as guards, alarm systems, and physical barriers to entry. You should take this seriously enough to train yourself in self-defense, and carry such legal defensive weapons with you as a shrill whistle, pepper spray, or Mace. There are many tips that you can obtain from a self-defense book or a class.

The greatest threat to your safety and that of your children is in your failure to take threats from your ex-husband seriously, thinking you can handle him the way you have always handled him. The graveyard is full of women who were of that view, and we don't want you to be added to the grim number.

III. WHAT IF THE ALIMONY OR CHILD SUPPORT PAYMENTS STOP

One of the meanest realities about divorce is that after all the pain, negotiating, fussing, and feuding, you finally get an award of alimony and child support—and when that's all over, that's when the real fight begins. You have the piece of paper that says so much support is to be paid, but try collecting it!

For reasons that we can't explain, many fathers are unwilling to support their own children. The result has been a national crisis, as desperate mothers try to track down and dun deadbeat dads, often without success. Fathers have been known to flee the state, to deliberately quit jobs, to go to jail, to change identities, and to utilize any number of devices to avoid paying money to their ex-spouses to enable them to put food in the mouths of their children.

Some psychologists have told us that this is really an attempt to punish the mother by burdening her with the total responsibility for the children. Most fathers know the mother would starve herself before letting the children go hungry. While punishment of the former spouse may be the intent, that is not the result. The result is a growing number of children living in poverty in the richest nation in the world.

It is estimated that 21 percent of all the children in the United States live in poverty. That statistic is in large measure due to deadbeat dads. Of course, the general public bears the brunt of these defalcations by fathers in that tax dollars are being used around the country to help these poverty-stricken children.

Probably one of the most dramatic examples of deadbeat dads was the case of John Gansalves, who had walked out on his wife, Marie Hines, in 1946, leaving behind three children ages two, four, and six. Marie ultimately got a divorce, alimony, and child support but was never able to find John or to collect any of that support. Ironically, they both continued to live in the same general area of southeastern Massachusetts and even saw each other occasionally. However, John never provided any support to help raise his three children or paid the court-ordered alimony. Marie raised the children by working two jobs and collecting some welfare. Finally, in August 1994, Marie, now seventy-three, went back to family court for an order that John, now seventy-one, pay forty-eight years of back alimony and child support. The two negotiated and agreed that he would pay her approximately $100,000. That wasn't hard for John, because he had just won the Massachusetts lottery jackpot of $5.1 million.

Public concern has grown so strong in some states that district attorneys are using police to track down deadbeat dads and jail them. However, this method of enforcement is sporadic and uneven, and the problem of deadbeat dads is still largely unsolved. If you have custody of the kids, be prepared to face the reality of deadbeat dads. Try to obtain some security for the payment of the support. Take the matter to court within a reasonable period of time after the first default. Obtain a wage assignment so his employer pays you directly.

The same is true of alimony. Fathers who want to punish ex-wives by hurting the children are certainly not going to be any more generous with their obligation to pay support to their former spouse. Here again, as we have noted, some ex-husbands will go to incredible lengths to duck paying alimony. It is a situation you have to live with, work out some guarantee of payment, or spend your life pursuing and suing.

IV. BEHAVIOR AFTER A DIVORCE

The marriage is over, but the relationship is not. That is a simple, but difficult truth for many to learn. After the divorce has been granted, your ex-spouse does not disappear from the face of the earth, as exciting as that concept might be. Your relationship with him continues in many different ways and at many different levels. You are no longer sleeping together (at least in most cases), but each affects the other's life through various contacts—your children, mutual friends, and perhaps family. Moreover, your relationship with your ex will always be subject to change as both of you grow older and your respective lives change; hopefully, your lives as well as your relationship will change for the better.

An important part of this changing but continuous relationship is that the final terms of the divorce are frequently *not* final. As each of your respective financial situations changes, for example, one or both of you may try to alter the financial obligations you have with each other. If the supporting ex-spouse gets a large increase in income, the receiving ex-spouse may want to get bigger payments. We have discussed the difficulties of obtaining such an order for modification in an earlier chapter. Conversely, if the supporting spouse suffers financial reverses, he or she may seek a reduction in alimony payments, a course of action much easier to obtain.

The behavior of each ex-spouse after divorce can also have an impact on the relationship. The supporting ex-spouse doesn't want to pay forever and will hope the supported ex-spouse will remarry and the alimony will terminate. This, as we have already noted, leads some receiving spouses to avoid the technical requirements of marriage and instead simply have a "roommate." If one spouse is suspected of child abuse, addicted to alcohol or drugs, a convicted criminal, a molester or rapist, or is involved in behavior that endangers the children, the other ex-spouse will often seek to terminate custody or visitation rights.

There have been too many cases where a former ex-spouse will kidnap the children, allegedly to protect them but more likely to hurt the other spouse, or in a drastic measure taken to eliminate child support payments. For example, many of the missing children whose photographs you see on milk cartons have been kidnapped by one of their parents. In the famous Morgan case in Washington, D.C., the mother kidnapped her daughter and smuggled her out of the country to live with the maternal grandparents in New Zealand. The mother charged the father with sexual molestation of the child. The mother went to jail for over a year for contempt of court when she refused to reveal the child's whereabouts to the judge.

In Texas, Chuck Smith spent most of an automobile dealership fortune he inherited in eight years of litigation for custody of his and his wife, Carolyn's, two sons. When she was awarded custody, he kidnapped the kids and fled to Mexico, where they remained for seven years. If the mother had not herself been wealthy, she might not have been able to hire the private detectives who finally located the father and the kidnapped children The father was arrested and returned to Texas for trial, where he was convicted of kidnapping. Such behavior is totally unacceptable and will damage the children as well as the parent left behind.

In 1994 Michelle Al-Naserri's two-year-old son was kidnapped by his father and Michelle's ex-husband, Haitham Khalid Al-Nasserri, who fled with the child to Iraq. After hiring a firm called Corporate Training Unlimited that specializes in recovering such kidnapped children from foreign countries, she was able to lure her ex-husband

and the child to London, where the ex-husband was arrested by Scotland Yard and the child, Laith-Adam, returned to Michelle.

This case focused on the kidnapping of a child by a parent who then takes the child to a foreign country. Not long before this case, a father murdered his ex-wife, the mother of his two children, in New Jersey and fled to Jordan. Ultimately the children were recovered and the father arrested by the Jordanian police. However, the U.S. State Department admits it has hundreds of such custody kidnap cases, and they are very rarely able to recover the children because of the laws and customs of the foreign country to which the children are taken.

And so it goes, endlessly. Again, the point is that the marriage is over, but the relationship isn't. Your behavior after the divorce can continue to severely affect the lives of those who were involved in the marriage, the ex-spouse, the children, other dependents, and other family members.

V. MEDICAL INSURANCE, TAXES, AND OTHER SPECIAL CONCERNS

A. Thank Goodness for COBRA

Today one of the major concerns for the citizens of the United States is health insurance. When you are no longer married to the wage earner who has insurance coverage through his job, you will be ineligible for coverage on his insurance plan. Of course, if you are the main income earner in the family, the reverse could be true. Fortunately, under a law passed by Congress several years ago with the tongue-twisting name of "The Consolidated Omnibus Budget Reconciliation Act," or COBRA, each divorced spouse is allowed to remain under the medical coverage of the other spouse's company for three years after the judgment. There is a limitation on the amount of premiums that the insurance company can charge during that three-year period, and there are a couple of cautions, as usual: COBRA only applies to companies with twenty or more employees that, obviously, have a health insurance program, and you may have to pay the premiums during those three years yourself unless you can negotiate that your ex-spouse pay. There are also some state variations on insurance coverage laws that your attorney should discuss with you.

B. Selling the Home and Other Real Estate

One of the assets that often is awarded to the wife is the family home, on the theory that she will have custody of the children and it is initially best if the children remain living in the same familiar place.

With the granting of the divorce decree, it seems logical that the wife might receive the home as part of the division of the real estate that had been owned jointly. However, there are several significant aspects in that logic that may cause some rethinking of what once seemed sensible; those are called mortgages and taxes.

1. *Mortgages.* If you retain the residence and it is put in your in name alone, you may be in for a nasty surprise. Many real estate mortgages have what is called an "acceleration" clause that says if the property changes ownership, the entire mortgage is due and payable immediately. So you may be in the position of negotiating a new mortgage. Since a single owner sometimes doesn't have the financial strength of a married couple, the terms of the new mortgage may be impossible, to the point of making you sell the property in a forced sale for whatever you can get for it.

If you decide to keep the property in both names, you could face other problems. If the two of you are to remain as joint owners of property, your fate is still inextricably bound with that of your ex-husband. You will have a continued relationship with your ex-spouse. He may decide to sell or refinance his share, forcing you to sell the property or to deal with other owners. Make sure your divorce decree precludes this. Or he might leave his share to his girlfriend or next wife, which could put you in an uncomfortable partnership with the "other woman." If he suffers financial reverses, his creditors can put liens on the property you jointly own, and you might be stuck with paying off debts he has incurred and refuses or is unable to pay. Again, make sure your divorce decree precludes this behavior.

You could try some tried and true escape routes, such as confirming the property to you in the judgment and obtaining a quit-claim deed from your ex to use whenever you need to refinance or dispose of the property. The problem may be that unless you record the quit-claim deed with the county recorder, you have not provided public notice of your sole ownership of the property. If you record the quit-claim deed, the mortgage company will pick up the recordation of the deed and you run the risk of the loan being called. Also, the quit-claim gimmick may be a criminal act, resulting in a fraud on the bank that could lead to some jail time. All in all, not a terribly smart move. In California, however, the method of quit-claiming property to one spouse is a useful device that has not usually resulted in acceleration of the loan. In the event of default in the payment by the in-house spouse, the other spouse is protected because the lending company can only look to the property to recoup its loan. Of course, foreclosure will damage the credit of whoever owes the debt.

2. *Taxes.* There are, of course, tax implications on divorce. If the real estate you are dividing is improved and not your residence, it can be depreciated; this is a valuable deduction from your income tax standpoint that can save either you or your ex-spouse tax money. This should have been figured in the total property settlement back in the trial.

Second, if you sell your home when you are fifty-five or older, you are entitled to a one-time-only exemption of the first $125,000 of capital gains from the sale. While you are married the exemption is limited to $125,000 for both husband and wife, so if you intend to sell and you are over age fifty-five, you must not close escrow until after the divorce.

There are also tax implications of the divorce settlement and in the payments between ex-spouses afterward. There are basically three kinds of money or property transfers between the ex-spouses after divorce: property division, child support, and alimony. As a rule, alimony is deductible from the payer's income, but is taxable for the ex-spouse receiving it. Child support, however, is the other way around in that the receiving spouse doesn't have to pay tax on it and the paying ex-spouse can't deduct it. A division of property, the third category, is not considered a taxable transaction. Of course, these tax laws suggest various ways of payment between ex-spouses that are the most tax advantageous.

C. Social Security

If you have been married for ten years or longer, when you reach retirement age you are entitled to one of two social security payment plans, that based on your earnings and that based on your husband's. In the old days of single wage-earner families, that was no contest because the husband's earnings was substantially higher or the wife had none at all. While women are in the work force in greater numbers today, there is still a substantial disparity between what a woman earns in a comparable job, so your own entitlement to social security will probably be less than your husband's.

If you decide that you are better off claiming through your ex-husband's social security, this will not cut down on what your ex will receive.

MAKING DIVORCE LESS PAINFUL

Some leading divorce attorneys have advice on making the divorce process less painful. New York City attorney Helen Brezinsky advises:

Rule 1: Compartmentalize feelings of anger and guilt and keep them out of negotiations. "A good deal has a lot to do with being reasonable about your expectations. Revenge is not a reasonable expectation." Many lawyers recommend that clients see a therapist while negotiating so as to have someplace to vent accumulated hostility before it robs them of all judgment.

Rule 2: Hire a good lawyer because the conflict is no longer over who is to blame, but who gets what property. Most courts think of marriage today as a financial partnership and want to split the property according to the concept called equitable distribution, which is the law in over forty states, with nine others using the community property or split fifty-fifty approach. Under equitable distribution laws, most states divide only assets acquired during marriage, except for separate property that you brought into the marriage or was given you or you inherited.

Finally, where you file for and obtain your divorce can have a bearing on how painful or speedy it is. Some tips about this include:

Nevada is still the queen of the quickie in terms of its popularity. It requires that you reside there six weeks, and then you can get a divorce in forty-eight hours. Alaska will let you file for divorce the day you arrive and then it may take a month or so to get the divorce. In contrast, most other states require you live there six months to a year before you can file for divorce.

Besides the time involved, whether you need to demonstrate grounds for divorce is an important factor. Some states require more proof and specific grounds than others. While many states now accept the vague charge of incompatibility, New York, South Carolina, and Virginia will not. In California all you have to cite is irreconcilable differences.

We said marriage was about love and divorce was about money, so if there is serious money involved, most spouses with big assets want to avoid residing in the nine community-property states of Arizona, California, Idaho, Louisiana, Nevada, New Mexico, Texas, Washington, and Wisconsin. They will probably do better in the other forty, equitable-distribution states and will do best in a state, of which there is only one, Mississippi, where title controls ownership.

Also when money matters, you want to check how the state regards separate property, such as gifts and inheritances. Twelve states, including Connecticut, Georgia, and Hawaii, throw gifts and inheritances into the common marital pot to be divided like everything else. And if you are the principal wage earner, you'll love being deep in the heart of Texas, where there is no alimony.

Unfortunately, there is no perfect place in the United States to get a divorce, but a little investigation, thought, and reasoning can mean a little less agony. In closing, we hope that this book will help you to prepare yourself for the eventuality of divorce, notwithstanding where you live, where you file, and what your assets are.

APPENDICES

I. SUMMARY OF DIVORCE LAWS IN THE FIFTY STATES

The following charts are reprinted with permission from *Family Law Quarterly* 27:4 (Winter 1994), published by the American Bar Association, Section of Family Law.

A. Alimony/Spousal Support Factors

	Statutory List	Marital Fault Not Considered	Marital Fault Relevant	Standard of Living	Status as Custodial Parent
Alabama			X		
Alaska	X	X		X	X
Arizona	X	X		X	X
Arkansas		X			
California		X			
Colorado	X	X		X	X
Connecticut	X		X	X	X
Delaware	X	X		X	X.
D.C.			X		
Florida	X		X	X	
Georgia	X		X	X	
Hawaii	X	X		X	X
Idaho	X		X		
Illinois	X	X		X	X
Indiana		X			X
Iowa	X	X		X	X
Kansas		X			
Kentucky	X	X		X	
Louisiana	X		X		X
Maine		X			
Maryland	X		X	X	
Massachusetts	X		X	X	X
Michigan					
Minnesota	X	X		X	X
Mississippi			X		
Missouri	X		X	X	X
Montana	X	X		X	X
Nebraska		X			
Nevada	X	X			
New Hampshire	X		X	X	X
New Jersey		X			
New Mexico		X			
New York	X	X			X
North Carolina		X	X		
North Dakota			X		
Ohio	X	X		X	X
Oklahoma		X			
Oregon	X	X		X	X
Pennsylvania	X		X	X	X
Rhode Island	X		X	X	
South Carolina			X		
South Dakota			X		
Tennessee	X		X	X	X
Texas		X			
Utah			X		
Vermont	X	X		X	X
Virginia	X		X	X	
Washington	X	X		X	
West Virginia			X		
Wisconsin	X	X			
Wyoming			X		

B. Custody Criteria

	Statutory Guidelines	Children's Wishes	Joint Custody Laws	Cooperative Parent	Domestic Violence	Health	Attorney or GAL for Child
Alabama	X		X				
Alaska	X	X	X	X	X	X	X
Arizona	X	X	X	X	X	X	X
Arkansas							
California	X	X	X		X		X
Colorado	X	X	X	X	X	X	X
Connecticut		X	X				X
Delaware	X	X				X	X
D.C.	X	X			X	X	X
Florida	X	X	X		X		X
Georgia	X	X	X				X
Hawaii	X	X			X		X
Idaho	X	X	X		X	X	
Illinois	X	X	X	X	X	X	X
Indiana	X	X	X				X
Iowa	X	X	X	X	X	X	X
Kansas	X	X	X	X	X	X	
Kentucky	X	X	X		X		X
Louisiana	X	X	X		X		
Maine	X	X			X		X
Maryland			X		X		X
Massachusetts			X		X		X
Michigan	X	X	X	X	X		X
Minnesota	X	X	X		X		X
Mississippi	X		X				
Missouri	X	X	X		X		X
Montana	X	X	X		X		X
Nebraska	X	X	X			X	X
Nevada	X	X	X		X		X
New Hampshire	X	X	X		X		X
New Jersey	X	X	X	X	X	X	X
New Mexico	X	X	X	X	X	X	X
New York		X	X				X
North Carolina		X	X				
North Dakota	X	X			X	X	X
Ohio	X	X	X		X	X	X
Oklahoma	X	X	X		X		
Oregon	X		X		X		X
Pennsylvania			X	X	X		X
Rhode Island			X		X		X
South Carolina		X	X				
South Dakota		X	X				X
Tennessee		X	X				
Texas		X	X		X	X	X
Utah	X	X	X				X
Vermont	X		X		X		X
Virginia	X		X			X	X
Washington	X	X			X	X	X
West Virginia		X	X		X		
Wisconsin	X	X	X	X	X	X	
Wyoming		X			X	X	

C. Child Support Guidelines

	Income Share	Percent of Income	Extraordinary Medical Formula	Child-Care Formula	Post-Majority Support
Alabama	X				X
Alaska		X			
Arizona	X				
Arkansas		X			
California	X		X	X	
Colorado	X		X	X	X
Connecticut	X				
Delaware			X	X	
D.C.					
Florida	X				
Georgia		X			
Hawaii					X
Idaho	X		X	X	
Illinois		X			X
Indiana	X		X	X	X
Iowa	X		X	X	
Kansas	X		X	X	
Kentucky	X				
Louisiana	X		X	X	
Maine	X		X	X	
Maryland	X		X	X	
Massachusetts					
Michigan	X		X	X	
Minnesota		X			
Mississippi		X			
Missouri	X				X
Montana			X	X	
Nebraska	X				
Nevada		X	X	X	
New Hampshire		X			
New Jersey	X		X	X	
New Mexico	X		X	X	
New York		X	X	X	
North Carolina	X		X	X	
North Dakota		X			
Ohio	X				
Oklahoma	X				
Oregon	X		X	X	
Pennsylvania	X				
Rhode Island	X				
South Carolina	X				X
South Dakota	X				
Tennessee		X			X
Texas		X			
Utah	X		X	X	
Vermont	X		X	X	
Virginia	X		X	X	
Washington	X		X	X	X
West Virginia			X	X	
Wisconsin		X			
Wyoming	X				

D. Grounds for Divorce and Residence Requirements

	No Fault Sole Ground	No Fault Added to Traditional	Incompatability	Living Separate and Apart	Judicial Separation or Maintenance	Durational Requirements
Alabama		X	X	2 years	X	6 months
Alaska		X	X		X	None
Arizona	X				X	90 days
Arkansas		X		18 months	X	60 days
California	X				X	6 months
Colorado	X				X	90 days
Connecticut		X		18 months	X	1 year
Delaware	X					6 months
D.C.	X			1 year	X	6 months
Florida	X					6 months
Georgia		X		1 year		6 months
Hawaii	X			2 years	X	6 months
Idaho		X			X	6 weeks
Illinois		X		2 years	X	90 days
Indiana		X			X	6 months
Iowa	X				X	None
Kansas			X		X	60 days
Kentucky	X				X	180 days
Louisiana		X		6 months	X	None
Maine		X			X	6 months
Maryland		X		2 years	X	1 year
Massachusetts		X			X	None
Michigan	X				X	6 months
Minnesota	X				X	180 days
Mississippi		X				6 months
Missouri	X				X	90 days
Montana	X		X	180 days	X	90 days
Nebraska	X				X	1 year
Nevada			X	1 year	X	6 weeks
New Hampshire		X		2 years		1 year
New Jersey		X		18 months	X	1 year
New Mexico		X	X			6 months
New York		X	X	1 year	X	1 year
North Carolina				1 year	X	6 months
North Dakota		X			X	6 months
Ohio		X	X	1 year		6 months
Oklahoma		X			X	6 months
Oregon	X				X	6 months
Pennsylvania		X		1 year		6 months
Rhode Island		X		3 years	X	1 year
South Carolina		X		1 year	X	1 year
South Dakota		X			X	None
Tennessee		X		2 years	X	6 months
Texas		X		3 years		6 months
Utah		X			X	90 days
Vermont		X		6 months		6 months
Virginia		X		1 year	X	6 months
Washington	X				X	1 year
West Virginia		X		1 year	X	1 year
Wisconsin	X			1 year	X	6 months
Wyoming	X				X	60 days

E. Property Division

	Community Property	Only Marital Property Divided	Statutory List of Factors	Nonmonetary Contributions	Economic Misconduct Considered	Special Contribution to Education
Alabama		X				
Alaska			X	X	X	X
Arizona	X		X			X
Arkansas		X	X	X		
California	X		X	X	X	X
Colorado		X	X	X	X	
Connecticut		X	X	X	X	X
Delaware			X	X	X	
D.C.		X	X	X	X	
Florida		X	X	X	X	X
Georgia		X				
Hawaii			X	X	X	
Idaho	X		X			
Illinois		X	X	X	X	
Indiana		X	X	X	X	
Iowa		X	X	X		X
Kansas			X		X	
Kentucky		X	X	X	X	X
Louisiana	X					
Maine		X	X	X		
Maryland		X	X	X		
Massachusetts			X	X		
Michigan						
Minnesota		X	X	X	X	
Mississippi						
Missouri		X	X	X		
Montana			X	X	X	
Nebraska		X		X		
Nevada	X					
New Hampshire			X	X	X	X
New Jersey		X	X	X		X
New Mexico	X					
New York		X	X	X	X	X
North Carolina		X	X	X	X	X
North Dakota				X		
Ohio		X	X	X	X	X
Oklahoma		X				
Oregon				X		
Pennsylvania		X	X	X	X	X
Rhode Island		X	X	X	X	X
South Carolina		X	X		X	X
South Dakota				X	X	
Tennessee		X	X	X	X	X
Texas	X				X	
Utah					X	
Vermont			X	X	X	X
Virginia		X	X	X		X
Washington	X		X			
West Virginia		X	X	X	X	X
Wisconsin	X		X	X		
Wyoming			X			

II. WOMEN'S BAR ASSOCIATIONS

These are resources for you in your state to obtain guidance to family law attorneys, support groups, clinics, and other assistance. Please keep in mind that these organizations change as new people are elected, and while the information given here is accurate as of the fall of 1994, some changes may have occurred by the time you read this. However, the organization names and locations can help you locate, through telephone directory assistance, any of the newer officials where that is necessary. We have indicated who the best contact person is for each of the associations listed.

Alabama

Mobile Bar Association—
  Women Lawyers Section
P.O. Drawer 2005
Mobile 36652
(205) 433-9790

Contact Person: Sandra
  Meadows
P.O. Box 16375
Mobile 36616
(205) 343-7717

Alaska

Anchorage Assn. of Women
  Lawyers
Contact Person: Marie Crosley
P.O. Box 104971
Anchorage 99510
(907) 278-6024

Arizona

Arizona Women Lawyers Assn.
1940 E. Thunderbird Road,
  # 103
Phoenix 85022
(602) 482-1827

Contact Person: Jean Gage
800 E. Wetmore Road #100
Tucson 85719-1550
(602) 292-4051

Arkansas

Arkansas Assn. of Women
  Lawyers
P.O. Box 95
Little Rock 72203-0095

Contact Person: Patty Lueken
217 W. Second Street
Little Rock 72201
(501) 374-0010

California

California Women Lawyers
Contact Person: Anita M. Miller
926 J Street, Suite 820
Sacramento 95814
(916) 441-3404

Black Women Lawyers Assn.
  of Los Angeles
Contact Person: Barbara R.
  Johnson
1 Manchester Blvd.
Inglewood 90301
(310) 412-5372

Black Women Lawyers Assn.
  of Northern California
Contact Person: Phyllis Culp
100 Van Ness Blvd., 28th floor
San Francisco 94102
(415) 241-2118

Contra Costa County Bar
  Assn.—Women's Section
Contact Person: Lisa Roberts
1211 Newell Avenue, 2nd floor
P.O. Box 5288
Walnut Creek 94596
(510) 939-3330

Inland Counties Woman at Law
Contact Person: Maryanne Carey
  Murphy
10126 Central Avenue, Suite B
Montclair 91763
(714) 625-0761

Kern County Women Lawyers
  Assn.
P.O. Box 691
Bakersfield 93301

Contact Person: Virginia
  Gennaro
1801 18th Street
Bakersfield 93301
(805) 327-5363

Lawyers Club of San Diego
Contact Person: Rebecca Michael
530 B Street, # 2300
San Diego 92101
(619) 234-0361

Marin County Women Lawyers
Contact Person: Wenden P.
  Treanor
1434 Lincoln Avenue
San Rafael 94901
(415) 258-0188

Contact Person: Lorena
  Chandler, Co-President
1299 Fourth Street, Suite
  405
San Rafael 94901
(415) 459-7283

Napa County Women Lawyers
Contact Person: Letty Van der
  Vegt
D.A. Family Support Division
P.O. Box 5720
Napa 94581
(707) 253-4355

Northern Santa Barbara County
  Women Lawyers
Contact Person: Soma F.
  Baldwin
301 E. Cook, Suite K-2
Santa Maria 93454
(805) 922-6155

Orange County Women Lawyers
  Association
Contact Person: Anita Miller
601 Civic Center Drive West
Santa Ana 92701
(714) 540-1047

Queen's Bench Bar Assn. of San
  Francisco Bay Area
Contact Person: Margaret A.
  Murray
505 Montgomery Street, 14th
  floor
San Francisco 94111
(415) 391-3333

Contact Person:
  Jill Schlichtmann
345 Franklin Street
San Francisco 94102
(415) 241-1937

Contact Person: Lisa Hamlin,
  Executive Secretary
333 Hayes Street, Suite 107
San Francisco 94102
(415) 863-2434

San Veranda Valley Women
  Lawyers Assn.
Contact Person: Deborah S.
  Myers
21800 Oxnard Street, Suite 450
Woodland Hills 91367
(818) 710-7777

San Francisco Women Lawyers
  Alliance
Contact Person: Ann G. Daniels
235 Montgomery Street
San Francisco 94104
(415) 954-4465

San Joaquin County Bar Assn.—
  Women Lawyer's Section
Contact Person: Judith K.
  Hansen
P.O. Box 8659
Stockton 95208
(209) 468-2730

San Joaquin County Bar Assn.
301 E. Weber Avenue
Stockton 95202
(209) 948-0125

San Mateo County Bar Assn.—
  Women Lawyer's Section
Contact Person: Leticia Toledo
700 El Camino Real
Millbrae 94030
(415) 871-5666

Santa Clara County Bar
  Assn./Women Lawyer's
  Committee
Contact Person: Kathryn K.
  Meier
60 S. Market Street, 14th floor
San Jose 95113
(408) 287-9501

Contact Person: Mary E. Tantillo
10 Almaden Blvd.
San Jose 95113
(408) 947-4000

Santa Clara County Bar Assn.
Contact Person: Christine
 Burdick
4 N. Second Street, Suite 400
San Jose 95113
(408) 287-2557

Solano County Women Lawyers,
 Inc.
Contact Person: Nancy M. Nolte
710 Missouri Street, Suite 3
Fairfield 94533
(707) 425-1058

Sonoma County Women in Law
Contact Person: Valorie Bader
P.O. Box 4112
Santa Rosa 95402-4112
(707) 542-2833

Stanislaus Country Women
 Lawyers
Contact Person: Susan D.
 Siefkin
1625 I Street
Modesto 95353
(209) 526-3500

Contact Person: Eve Fisher
P.O. Box 480197
Los Angeles 90048
(213) 653-3325

Women Lawyers Assn. of San
 Luis Obispo County
Contact Person: Angie King
1411 Marsh Street, Suite 201
San Luis Obispo 93401
(805) 541-2901

Women Lawyers of Alameda
 County
Contact Person: Gillian Ross
P.O. Box 2047
Oakland 94604
(510) 601-5600

Women Lawyers of Long Beach
Contact Person: Jane H. Benson
P.O. Box 21457
Long Beach 90801
(213) 624-8407

Women Lawyers of Placer
 County
Contact Person: Vicki Kalman
10563 Brunswick, Suite 7
Grass Valley 95945
(916) 272-9600

Women Lawyers of Sacramento
Contact Person: Tami J. Buscho
P.O. Box 161523
Sacramento 95816
(916) 348-2032

Women Lawyers of Santa Cruz
 County
Contact Person: Cindy Starr
129 Jewell Street
Santa Cruz 95060
(408) 458-9000

Women Lawyers of Ventura
 County
Contact Person: Elizabeth
 Capehart
1331 Cypress Point Lane,
 Suite 205
Ventura 93003
(805) 893-8027

Colorado

Colorado Women's Bar Assn.
1801 Broadway, # 350
Denver 80202
(303) 298-1313

Contact Person: Mary M. Phillips
303 East 17th Avenue, Suite 700
Denver 80203
(303) 830-0612

Boulder Women's Bar Assn.
Contact Person: Jenna
  Remington
P.O. Box 3004
Boulder 80203
(303) 447-1972

National Assn/Black Women
  Attorneys—Colorado Chapter
Contact Person: Carolyn Lievers
Office of the Attorney General
110 16th Street, 10th floor
Denver 80203
(303) 620-4500

Connecticut

Connecticut Bar Assn.—Women
  and the Law Section
101 Corporate Place
Rocky Hill 06067
(203) 721-0025

Contact Person: Gail Stern
162 Bishop Street
New Haven 06511

Hartford Assn. of Women
  Attorneys
Contact Person: Laura Gold
  Becker
One Corporate Center
Hartford 06103
(203) 523-6645

Contact Person: Jane Seidl
107 Seldon Road
Berlin 06037
(203) 665-5051

Delaware

Delaware State Bar Assn.—
  Section on Women and the
  Law
Contact Person: Nell S. Maier
902 Market Street, # 1300
Wilmington 19889
(302) 655-5000

Contact Person: Joanne M.H.
  Shalk
1220 Market Building
P.O. Box 410
Wilmington 19899
(302) 652-8400

District of Columbia

Women's Bar Assn. of D.C.
Contact Person: Kaye Hearn
1819 H Street NW, #1250
Washington, DC 20006
(202) 785-1540

National Bar Assn.—Women
    Lawyer's Division
Contact Person: Grace E.
    Speights
1800 M Street N.W.
Washington, DC 20036
(202) 467-7189
Contact Person: Cheryl Ziegler
8926 Hillside Court
Landover, Maryland 20785
(202) 514-8033

Florida

Florida Assn. for Women
    Lawyers
Contact Person: Sherri Gay
P.O. Box 10617
Tallahassee 32302
(904) 561-6344

Central Florida Assn. for Women
    Lawyers
Contact Person: Margaret H.
    Schreiber
215 N. Eola Drive
Orlando 32801
(407) 843-4600

Florida Assn. for Women
    Lawyers—Dade County
    Chapter
Contact Person: Gail L.
    Grossman
1481 NW North River Drive
Miami 33125
(305) 324-4443

Georgia

Georgia Assn. for Women
    Lawyers
999 Peachtree Street NE
Atlanta 30309-3996
(404) 853-8298

Hawaii

Hawaii Women Lawyers
P.O. Box 2072
Honolulu 96805

Idaho

Idaho Women Lawyers
P.O. Box 1683
Boise 83701

Illinois

Women's Bar Assn. of Illinois
309 West Washington, # 900
Chicago 60606
(312) 541-0048

Indiana

Indianapolis Bar Assn.—Women
    Lawyers Division
P.O. Box 2086
Indianapolis 46206-2086
(317) 269-2000

Iowa

Iowa Organization of Women
  Attorneys
P.O. Box 65852
West Des Moines 50265

Kansas

Wichita Women Lawyers
Wichita Bar Assn.
700 Epic Center
301 North Main
Wichita 67202
(316) 263-2251

Kentucky

Kentucky Bar Assn. for Women
2700 Citizens Plaza
Louisville 40202
(502) 589-5235

Louisiana

Louisiana Assn. for Women
  Attorneys
1126 Whitney Bank Building
228 St. Charles Avenue
New Orleans 70130
(504) 525-8832

Maine

Maine State Bar Assn.
1 Monument Square
Portland 04101
(207) 773-6411

Maryland

Women's Bar Assn of Maryland
520 East Fayette Street
Baltimore 21201
(410) 528-9681

Massachusetts

Women's Bar Assn.
  of Massachusetts
25 West Street, 4th floor
Boston 02111
(617) 695-1851

Michigan

Women Lawyers Assn.
  of Michigan
P.O. Box 26245
Lansing 48909-6245
(517) 487-3332

Minnesota

Minnesota Women Lawyers
513 Nicollet Mall
Minneapolis 55402
(612) 338-3205

Mississippi

Mississippi Woman's Lawyer
  Assn.
P.O. Box 862
Jackson 39205-0862

Missouri

Assn. of Women Lawyers of
    Greater Kansas City
P.O. Box 414557
Kansas City 64141

Montana

State Bar of Montana—Women's
    Law Section
P.O. Box 577
Helena 59624
(406) 442-7660

Nebraska

Nebraska State Bar Assn.—
    Women and the Law Section
P.O. Box 81809
635 S. 14th Street
Lincoln 68501-1809
(402) 475-7091

Nevada

Northern Nevada Women-
    Lawyers Assn.
350 S. Center Street, #530
Reno 89501
(702) 322-8999

New Hampshire

Hillsborough County Women's
    Bar Assn.
Contact Person: Julie Johnson
P.O. Box 915
Manchester 03105-0915
(603) 669-5000

New Jersey

New Jersey Women Lawyers
    Assn.
1200 Laurel Oak Road,#100
Voorhees 08043
(609) 627-4954

New Mexico

New Mexico Women's Bar Assn.
P.O. Drawer 887
Albuquerque 87103
(505) 842-8255

New York

Women's Bar Assn. of State of
    New York
246 Fifth Avenue, # 2103
New York City 10016
(212) 889-7813

North Carolina

North Carolina Assn. of Women
  Attorneys
P.O. Box 28121
Raleigh 27611-8121
(919) 833-4055, ext. 34

Ohio

Greater Cincinnati Women
  Lawyers Assn.
P.O. Box 3764
Cincinnati 45201-3764

Oklahoma

Oklahoma Assn. of Women
  Lawyers
Oklahoma Supreme Court
State Capitol
Oklahoma City 73102
(405) 521-2163

Oregon

Oregon Women Lawyers
P.O. Box 40393
Portland 97240
(503) 775-9021

Pennsylvania

NBA Women Lawyers Division
P.O. Box 58004
Philadelphia 19103

Rhode Island

Rhode Island Women's Bar Assn.
55 Dorrance Street
Providence 02903
(401) 331-3800

Tennessee

Tennessee Lawyers' Assn. for
  Women
P.O. Box 2813
Nashville 37219

Texas

State Bar Assn. of Texas
Women and the Law
P.O. Box 12487
Capitol Station
Austin 78711
(512) 463-1463

Utah

Women Lawyers of Utah
University of Utah/College of Law
Salt Lake City 84112
(801) 581-4661

Vermont

Vermont Bar Assn.—Women's
    Section
P.O. Box 100
Montpelier 05601
(802) 223-2020

Virginia

Virginia Women Attorneys Assn.
2nd & Franklin Street, # 405
Richmond 23219
(804) 775-2431

Washington State

Washington Women Lawyers
P.O. Box 25444
Seattle 98125-2344
(206) 622-5585

Wisconsin

Assn. for Women Lawyers
777 E. Wisconsin Avenue
Milwaukee 53202
(414) 289-3534

III. BOOKS AND COMPUTER SOFTWARE TO HELP YOU

Here are some books and computer software that might be helpful or of interest or both:

- *The Divorce Workbook: A Guide for Kids and Families.*
- *Divorce Yourself: The National No-Fault No-Lawyer Divorce Handbook,* by Daniel Sitarz.
- *Divorce: An American Tradition,* by Glenda Riley.
- *Divorce: An Attorney Tells You What You Should Know* (video recording).
- *Divorce and Dissolution of Marriage Laws of the United States,* by Daniel Sitarz.
- *Divorce and Money: Everything You Need to Know About Dividing Property,* by Violet Woodhouse, Victoria Felton-Collins, and M.C. Blakeman.
- *Divorce and New Beginnings: An Authoritative Guide to Recovery and Growth, Solo Parenting and Stepfamilies,* by Genevieve Clapp.
- *Divorce: Beginning the Journey* (video recording), by Mary Huzinec.
- *Divorce: Getting the Best Deal,* by Tricia Welsh and Julie Connelly.

Divorce Computer Software

Software Program Aids in Calculating Effects of a Divorce, by Michael D. Koppel.

FinPlan's (Chicago, IL) *Divorce Planner* is a spreadsheet template program that evaluates the tax effects of a divorce and calculates cash and tax flow results.

Divorce Planner is a stand-alone program that was originally a Lotus 1-2-3 template and that still uses Lotus commands. The program is menu driven, controlled by pull-down menus, and requires a hard disk. The spreadsheet is large and offers twelve different reports, including tax planner output, cash flow output, and present value of alimony. *Divorce Planner* is a powerful divorce tax-planning tool and includes many useful features, including a capacity to view alternative treatments side by side, and a model of home sales.

IV. DIVORCE SUPPORT GROUPS

Academy of Family Mediators
P.O. Box 10501
Eugene, Oregon 97440
(503) 345-1205
    Referrals to 2,000 profes-
sional mediators nationwide.

American Assn. for Marriage
    and Family Therapy
1100 17th Street N.W., 10th
    floor
Washington, DC 20036
(800) 374-2638
    Provides referrals for therapy
for single parents and step-
parents.

Assn. for Children for Enforce-
    ment of Support
723 Phillips Avenue
Toledo, Ohio 43612
(800) 537-7072
    Advice about getting child
support payments.

Committee for Mother and
    Child Rights
210 Old Orchard Drive
Clear Brook, Virginia 22624
(703) 722-3652
    Advice on custody or visita-
tion problems.

Divorce Anonymous
2600 Colorado Avenue, Suite 270
Santa Monica, California 90404
(310) 998-6538
    Has groups in eight states and
uses the twelve-step program
to help attendees through
divorce. More groups are
forming all the time.

Joint Custody Association
10606 Wilkins Avenue
Los Angeles, California 90024
(310) 475-5352
    Will send kit on joint custody.

Mothers Without Custody
P.O. Box 27418
Houston, Texas 77227
(713) 840-1622
    National organization with
$20 per year dues that
includes a newsletter and connection to a local chapter.

National Action for Former Mili-
    tary Wives
1700 Legion Drive
Winter Park, Florida 32789
(407) 628-2801
    Advice for former military
wives on benefits and rights
after they get a divorce.

National Center on Women and
Family Law
799 Broadway, Room 402
New York, New York 10003
   Send them a self-addressed
   stamped envelope and ask for
   information packets on either
   custody, support, or battered
   women.

North American Conference of
Separated & Divorced
Catholics
80 Saint Mary's Drive
Cranston, Rhode Island 02920
(401) 943-7903
   Can guide you to local support group in your town and
   state. There are groups in
   almost every diocese.

NOW Legal Defense and Education Fund
99 Hudson Street
New York, New York 10013
(212) 925-6635
   Will send you, for $5 each,
   kits on divorce and separation; child support, or child
   custody, explaining legal and
   financial aspects.

Parents Without Partners
8807 Colesville Road
Silver Spring, Maryland 20910
(800) 637-7974
   650 chapters around the
   country for single men and
   women who are parents. Telephone or send a stamped, self-
   addressed envelope and they
   will send you information
   with connection number for a
   chapter near you.

Stepfamily Association
of America
215 Centennial Mall South, Suite
212
Lincoln, Nebraska 68508
(402) 477-7837
   Over fifty groups nationally.
   Membership is $35 a year,
   with newsletter and catalog of
   books on remarriage and stepfamilies.

Stepfamily Foundation
333 West End Avenue
New York, New York 10023
(800) 759-7837
   Gives you information and
   counseling on the phone. Has
   a lecture bureau, books,
   videos, and newsletter. Membership is $65 a year.

Women on Their Own
P.O. Box 1026
Willingboro, New Jersey 08046
(609) 871-1499
   This is a national network of
   several hundred women who
   help each other with work,
   home sharing, child care, and
   other support. To join it costs
   $15 a year.

V. RECENT FAMILY LAW COURT RULINGS ON VARIOUS SUBJECTS

This sampling of family law court rulings on various subjects will illustrate the wide diversity of rulings possible from state to state and circumstance to circumstance.

Family Law in the Fifty States— Basis for Alimony *

View of Recent Cases in Various States

- ARKANSAS
  In *Busby v. Busby*, the court looked beyond the couple's net income to their total earning ability and the ill health of the wife. It ordered the husband to pay $35 a week in alimony even though the wife already received $1200 a month in benefits because she had bone cancer, no job, and heavy medical expenses.

- VERMONT
  Downs v. Downs involved a doctor husband and considered the future benefits of his degree, repayment of school loans, and buying into a medical partnership in setting the alimony. An important factor cited was the standard of living each spouse had and said the wife was entitled to more than just enough to meet her needs.

- IOWA
  In the Weiss case, the court took into consideration the inherited and gifted property of each of the spouses. Even though that is separate property and not subject to division between the divorcing spouses, the court used the property as a measure of whether or not alimony was appropriate or necessary.

  * *Interpretations of the law vary from state to state and from time to time. These views are only illustrations, and you should check with current rulings in your own state.*

Family Law in the Fifty States— More on Alimony Criteria *

View of Recent Cases in Various States

- MAINE
  In *Gray v. Gray*, the court said that the very high lifestyle of the couple during marriage justified alimony, even if the alimony-receiving spouse already had a good income.

- MISSISSIPPI
  The court outlined the factors it considered in deciding whether or not to award alimony. Those factors included: both parties' income and expenses; earning capacities; fault or misconduct; needs and obligations; age; length of the marriage; whether or not there were children; tax consequences; and if there had been an intemperate waste of the marriage's assets.

- MONTANA AND NEW MEXICO
  In both states, need was considered the main criterion in awarding alimony. In the Eschenbacher case, the Montana court awarded the wife $800 a month for eighteen months, even though the marriage was less than a year old, because the wife was poor and unable to support herself. In the New Mexico case of *Hall v. Hall*, the court simply said that the first criterion in determining alimony was need.

Interpretations of the law vary from state to state and from time to time. These views are only illustrations, and you should check with current rulings in your own state.

Family Law in the Fifty States—
Alimony Denied *

View of Recent Cases in Various States

- INDIANA
  In the Richmond case, the wife had asked for spousal support on the grounds that she was agoraphobic and afraid to leave the house. The court said that the evidence showed she functioned well enough to support and take care of herself and refused her request for support.

- MISSOURI
  In *Camden v. Camden*, the trial court denied temporary spousal support for the wife because she failed to show that she didn't have enough property to take of her needs or that she was unable to get a job and support herself.

- WEST VIRGINIA
  In *Channell v. Channell*, the court denied alimony to the wife because it found that both had about the same earning ability and only occasionally had worked, living most of the time off money the husband's family gave them.

Interpretations of the law vary from state to state and from time to time. These views are only illustrations, and you should check with current rulings in your own state.

Family Law in the Fifty States—
Rehabilitive Alimony *

View of Recent Cases in Various States

- ALASKA
  In *Renfro v. Renfro,* the court awarded the wife $400 a month in spousal support for forty-eight months so she could finish getting her degree in psychology.

- COLORADO
  In the Nordahl case, the appellate court ruled it was wrong to set a six-month limit on alimony after the wife completed her college undergraduate degree. That wasn't enough time for her to become fully self-sufficient.

- ILLINOIS
  In the Gunn case, the court awarded the forty-four-year-old wife $4,000 a month alimony until she was sixty based on the length of the marriage, her inability to support herself, her age, her lack of job skills, and the standard of living they had during marriage. However, in the Courtright case the court ruled that the alimony-receiving spouse was obligated to work and support herself, which she had failed to do for two years.

* Interpretations of the law vary from state to state and from time to time. These views are only illustrations, and you should check with current rulings in your own state.

Family Law in the Fifty States—
Reimbursement Alimony *
View of Recent Cases in Various States

- NORTH DAKOTA
  In *Culver v. Culver,* the court upheld on appeal alimony of $1,000 a month for ten years because the wife had accepted an austere and difficult life so the husband could complete two years of undergraduate college work, five years of medical school, and three years of residency. When he finally became a medical doctor, he left her, and the court said she was entitled to a payback for putting him through medical school.

- OHIO
  In the *Moro v. Moro* case, the court ruled that the wife of thirty-five years whose husband outearned her two to one, and had no pension, was entitled to five years of alimony.

- OKLAHOMA
  In *Forristall v. Forristall,* the court said that since the student loans taken out to finance her husband's medical education were joint debts, she was entitled to be reimbursed for her investment in her husband's medical degree in the form of alimony.

Interpretations of the law vary from state to state and from time to time. These views are only illustrations, and you should check with current rulings in your own state.

Family Law in the Fifty States—
Permanent Alimony *
View of Recent Cases in Various States

- ALASKA
  The court in *Jones v. Jones* preferred rehabilitative alimony, but awarded permanent alimony where the spouse didn't have a reasonable chance of supporting herself.

- CONNECTICUT
  In *Puris v. Puris,* the appellate court upheld permanent alimony to the wife of $276,000 a year, with the provision that it be reviewed when the husband retired.

- KENTUCKY
  The court refused permanent alimony in *Perrine v. Christine* to a wife in her late fifties, married thirty-four years who couldn't work, because her share of the marital property invested at 9 percent would provide her a lifetime annual income of $48,000.

- COLORADO
  In the Huff case, the court award the wife alimony of $5,000 a month that was to be reduced $1,000 a month every second year until it reached $1,000. That would continue until she died or remarried. The court said she was entitled to the same standard of living as before.

* Interpretations of the law vary from state to state and from time to time. These views are only illustrations, and you should check with current rulings in your own state.

Family Law in the Fifty States—
More Permanent Alimony *
View of Recent Cases in Various States

- CALIFORNIA
  The court of appeals in the Baker case ordered permanent alimony from the husband to the wife to support the same opulent lifestyle the couple enjoyed during their seven-year marriage, since the wife was unable to support herself. In another similar case, the court denied permanent alimony because the marriage was less than four years long.

- CONNECTICUT
  In the Vendredi case, the wife didn't speak English well, had limited and sporadic work as a seamstress, and was fifty years old with a limited education. The court awarded permanent alimony to sustain the very high standard of living the couple had enjoyed during marriage.

- UTAH
  The court of appeals ruled that the criteria for deciding on permanent alimony was whether the receiving party can work and support herself or himself at the same level of living standard as while married. In *Watson v. Watson*, the court awarded $2,000 a month for two years and $1,500 a month in permanent alimony thereafter.

Interpretations of the law vary from state to state and from time to time. These views are only illustrations, and you should check with current rulings in your own state.

Family Law in the Fifty States—
More Permanent Alimony *
View of Recent Cases in Various States

- IOWA

  The appellate court reversed the lower court in the case of Benson, in which the lower court had awarded $1 in alimony to a thirty-seven-year-old wife married seven years. Instead, the appellate court awarded her $300 a month since she was in poor health, couldn't support herself, and had custody of their four handicapped children.

- MISSISSIPPI

  The apellate court ruled the lower court was wrong to put a cut-off date on alimony in the *Cleveland v. Cleveland* case because future need could not be anticipated and the wife should have sufficient support to sustain herself as long as the husband can afford it.

- MISSOURI

  In *Wallace v. Wallace* the lower court was wrong when it refused alimony to a fifty-one-year-old sick wife on welfare and to the wife in the Smith case where the wife was totally disabled from arthritis.

  *Interpretations of the law vary from state to state and from time to time. These views are only illustrations, and you should check with current rulings in your own state.

Family Law in the Fifty States—
Collecting from Nonpayers *
View of Recent Cases in Various States

- ARIZONA
  The appellate court ordered the husband's workman's compensation benefits attached to pay back alimony in *Brooks v. Consolidated Freightways.*

- KANSAS
  The court ruled in *Dozier v. Dozier* that failure to pay court-ordered alimony was willful disobedience of a court order and would result in jail time. It dismissed the argument that this would be unconstitutionally jailing a person for nonpayment of a debt.

Interpretations of the law vary from state to state and from time to time. These views are only illustrations, and you should check with current rulings in your own state.

Family Law in the Fifty States—
Effect of Income Changes *
View of Recent Cases in Various States

- ALABAMA
  The court of appeals in *Maddox v. Maddox* refused to reduce the alimony a husband had to pay just because he had voluntarily retired. It noted that his ability to earn had not decreased and he had other assets from which to pay.

- CALIFORNIA
  In one case, Meegan, the alimony was cut to zero because the husband had quit his high-paying job and, in good faith, become a priest. In the other case, Ilas, the husband quit his job as a pharmacist to go to medical school and wanted alimony and child support reduced. That was denied by the court.

- OREGON
  In the Haywood case, the wife remarried, but wanted to continue getting alimony from her previous husband on the grounds that she and her new husband did not commingle incomes and the new husband didn't contribute fully to the marriage financially. The appellate court terminated the alimony from the previous husband.

  Interpretations of the law vary from state to state and from time to time. These views are only illustrations, and you should check with current rulings in your own state.

Family Law in the Fifty States—
Modifying Divorce Terms *
View of Recent Cases in Various States

- ARKANSAS
  In *Smith v. Smith,* the husband petitioned the court to terminate his obligation to pay alimony because his wife had remarried and the court refused.

- CALIFORNIA
  The appellate court refused to modify its order that the wife receive alimony for life or until remarriage just because the husband died. The marital settlement required the husband maintain life insurance to guarantee that. Since he did not, his estate must continue paying the alimony.

- MONTANA
  In the McKeon case, the husband petitioned for a modification of the divorce terms on the grounds that the court's order that he pay his ex-wife $300 a month "for life" was vague and uncertain. The court disagreed and said that "for life" was clear and unambiguous and he had to keep on paying.

*Interpretations of the law vary from state to state and from time to time. These views are only illustrations, and you should check with current rulings in your own state.

Family Law in the Fifty States— Remarriage or Cohabitation *

View of Recent Cases in Various States

- IOWA
  The court ordered alimony of $3,500 a month for ten years in the Gillilland case as a way to allow the wife to become self-supporting, and it refused to terminate this spousal support just because the wife remarried.

- OHIO
  The Ohio appellate court reversed the lower court in *Perri v. Perri,* which had terminated spousal support because the wife was living with another man. In order for the support to be ended, the court said, it would have to be proven that the alimony was used for the live-in lover's support.

- WEST VIRGINIA
  The court in *McVay v. McVay* cut the ex-wife's alimony from $876.06 a month to $1 a year because she had started living with another man. The court of appeals reversed that ruling, saying the lower court shouldn't have focused on the cohabitation, but on her changed financial circumstances if she had found work or the lover was paying part of her bills.

Interpretations of the law vary from state to state and from time to time. These views are only illustrations, and you should check with current rulings in your own state.

Family Law in the Fifty States—
Court Custody Jurisdiction *
View of Recent Cases in Various States

- VIRGINIA
  While the divorce action was pending in *Lutes v. Alexander*, the father took the children to a foreign country for fifteen years. The Virginia court of appeals ruled that Virginia courts still had jurisdiction over the case and custody of the children.

- WASHINGTON STATE
  In the Ieronimakis case, the parents were living in Greece, the native country of the father, and the children were all born there. When the marriage came apart, the mother, an American citizen, returned to the state of Washington with the children and filed for divorce. Washington courts ruled that the custody of the children should be decided by the Greek courts.

  Interpretations of the law vary from state to state and from time to time. These views are only illustrations, and you should check with current rulings in your own state.

Family Law in the Fifty States—
Custody Awarding Criteria *
View of Recent Cases in Various States

- ARIZONA
  In lower court in the *Montoya v. Superior Court* case, the father refused to answer questions about his past drug addiction and the court awarded custody of the child to the mother without further hearing. The appellate court overturned that, saying the court must spell out why the decision was in the best interests of the child.

- MISSISSIPPI
  The court in *Faries v. Faries* set out its criteria for awarding child custody: "The polestar consideration is the best interest and welfare of the child." Other factors included sex of the child; which parent was main caretaker; parenting skills; physical and mental health of parents; stability of the home; and, preference of the child if old enough legally to express such preference.

- NEW YORK
  In *Ramshaw v. Ramshaw,* the appellate court awarded the custody of a three-year-old child to the mother while directing her to get counseling to enable her to be more relaxed and less compulsive with the infant.

  * Interpretations of the law vary from state to state and from time to time. These views are only illustrations, and you should check with current rulings in your own state.

Family Law in the Fifty States— Who's Primary Caretaker? *

View of Recent Cases in Various States

- IOWA
  In the Fennell case, the court awarded the custody to the stay-at-home father who couldn't earn a living even though the mother had an excellent job history.

- NEW YORK
  In *Bohnsack v. Bohnsack,* the mother was awarded custody because she was the major psychological parent as well as the central attachment figure in the children's lives. However, in *McGrew v. Chase*, the father got custody because he adjusted work hours to spend more time with the children, had a nice house, and did the house cleaning, feeding, bathing, and caring for the children before the separation. The neighbors testified that the mother was neither a good mother nor a good housekeeper.

- WASHINGTON STATE
  The court ruled in the Kovacs case that just because one is the primary caretaker of the child does not automatically mean it was in the best interests of the child to give custody to that parent. There are, the court said, many factors to consider as it awarded the custody of the three children to the father.

  Interpretations of the law vary from state to state and from time to time. These views are only illustrations, and you should check with current rulings in your own state.

Family Law in the Fifty States—
Wishes of the Children *

View of Recent Cases in Various States

- ILLINOIS
  In the Anderson matter, the trial court was going to award custody of a fourteen-year-old son to his mother but changed it to his father, based on the child's wish to live with his father.

- MICHIGAN AND MONTANA
  In cases in each of these states (*Treutle v. Treutle*) (*In re Black*), neither judge consulted the children's wishes, and that was ruled proper because the children were considered too young to make a considered judgment.

- TENNESSEE
  In *Harris v. Harris,* the judge spoke in private with the minor child involved who vigorously objected living with her mother. As a result, the court ruled that the mother could get custody only if she could prove that the father was unfit.

  * Interpretations of the law vary from state to state and from time to time. These views are only illustrations, and you should check with current rulings in your own state.

Family Law in the Fifty States—
Parental Cooperation *
View of Recent Cases in Various States

- NEW YORK
In the case of *Marie B. v. Karranchard B.*, the court awarded custody to the mother because she demonstrated that she respected the children's relationship with their father. In contrast, the father blatantly attempted to manipulate everyone and brainwash the children against their mother. In contrast, in *McGrew v. Chase*, the mother maliciously and inaccurately charged the father with child abuse. The court awarded the children to the father after testimony of the neighbors and older children proved that the reverse was true and that the mother was abusive and sought to deny the father visitation rights to the children.

- ALASKA
After the couple separated, the mother moved to Norway with the child, refused the father all visits and correspondence with the child, and was totally uncooperative with the court, leading the court to award custody of the child to the father. The Supreme Court reversed that custody award in *Hakas v. Bergenthal* on the grounds that custody must be awarded on the basis of what is best for the child irrespective of the cooperation or lack of cooperation of either parent.

Interpretations of the law vary from state to state and from time to time. These views are only illustrations, and you should check with current rulings in your own state.

Family Law in the Fifty States—
Abuse and Violence *
View of Recent Cases in Various States

- ALABAMA
  In *E. W. v. Montgomery County Department of Human Resources,* medical evidence of sexual abuse was presented to the court along with the testimony of the children, and this resulted in custody being taken away from the father.

- NEW YORK
  In the case of *Graci v. Graci,* the mother filed an unsubstantiated charge of sexual misconduct against the father; she was, however, awarded custody anyhow. The court said on appeal a parent's prior misconduct was important only if it affected that parent's ability to be a good mother or father to the child. Custody, it said, should not be used to punish the misbehaving parent, and in this case the mother had the better home environment and could better provide for their religious upbringing.

  * Interpretations of the law vary from state to state and from time to time. These views are only illustrations, and you should check with current rulings in your own state.

Family Law in the Fifty States—
Other Custody Factors *
View of Recent Cases in Various States

- TENDER YEARS DOCTRINE
  Under the long-standing "tender years doctrine," the theory has been that very young children are best in the custody of their mother. In the South Carolina case of *Wheeler v. Gill,* the court said the doctrine is used as a tiebreaker when both parents are equally fit, and the Tennessee case of *Malone v. Malone* directed that this be a factor in determining custody.

- RELIGION
  Religion has come to play less of a role in the determination of child custody. The Colorado court (*In re Oswald*) said the court cannot restrict the religious upbringing either parent gives a child. The Maryland court said that religion alone cannot be a factor in custody unless it has some bearing on the physical or emotional welfare of the child.

- SEPARATION OF CHILDREN
  In most cases, the courts prefer not to break up siblings. That was held true in recent cases in Maine (*Daigle v. Daigle*); Maryland (*Hadick v. Hadick*); and, New York (*Lee v. Halayko*).

  * Interpretations of the law vary from state to state and from time to time. These views are only illustrations, and you should check with current rulings in your own state.